Boom Baby

Boom Baby

Natalie Meisner

Boom Baby
first published 2025 by Scirocco Drama
An imprint of J. Gordon Shillingford Publishing Inc.

Scirocco Drama Editor: Glenda MacFarlane
Cover design by Doowah Design
Cover photo by Tim Nguyen, Fifth Wall Media
Author photo of Natalie Meisner by Lori Maloney Photography
Production photos by Morgan Laidley

Printed and bound in Canada on 100% post-consumer recycled paper.

Production inquiries:
nmeisner@mtroyal.ca
https://nataliemeisner.com

Library and Archives Canada Cataloguing in Publication

Title: Boom baby / Natalie Meisner.
Names: Meisner, Natalie, 1972- author.
Identifiers: Canadiana 20250259575 | ISBN 9781990738753 (softcover)
Subjects: LCGFT: Drama.
Classification: LCC PS8576.E433 B66 2025 | DDC C812/.54—dc23

We acknowledge the financial support of the Canada Council for the Arts, the Government of Canada, the Manitoba Arts Council, and the Manitoba Government for our publishing program.

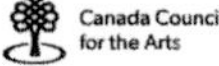

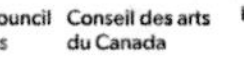

J. Gordon Shillingford Publishing
P.O. Box 86, RPO Corydon Avenue, Winnipeg, MB Canada R3M 3S3

*I dedicate this to Pamela Halstead and Jason Mehmel,
two of the finest theatre collaborators I have had the honour
of working with.*

Natalie Meisner

Natalie Meisner is a professor, a playwright, a poet, a mom, and now a podcast host (not necessarily always in that order). She was born on the Mi'kma'ki / south shore of Nova Scotia where she began her curious life by reading, with wild abandon, all the books that came through in the town bookmobile. She has seven full-length books in various genres to her name, was Calgary / Mohkinstsis's fifth Poet Laureate, and teaches creative writing at Mount Royal University, where she loves helping other writers find their voices.

www.nataliemeisner.com

Acknowledgements

At the first rehearsal of the SAGE production, Jason called us the *Boom Baby Family.* By this I believe he also meant to acknowledge every actor, director, dramaturge, producer, creative, or audience member who has been part of the show's growth to date. This is indeed a fitting and beautiful way to conceive of theatre: a kind of chosen family that stretches across the city, across the country and sometimes even across the oceans. We come to the theatre to grapple with some of the toughest and most complex questions facing us as a society, but we do it together. Thank you for becoming a part of the *Boom Baby* as you read (or stage) the play.

I want to give thanks to every single actor who has contributed to a reading or staging of *Boom Baby*—you have left your prints on it. Also, I give thanks for every director, producer, and designer who has had a hand in bringing the play to the stage. A theatre script is nothing more than a blueprint, no matter how crafty or exquisite, until we bring it to life together. I also treasure greatly the keen editorship and intellect of the first readers, editors, and dramaturges who have helped me find the sharp edges and the warmest places in this text. Dianne Richards, Pamela Halstead, Kathleen Tudor, Chapelle Jaffe, Carolyn Zapf, Kristine Greenaway, Mary-Barnes Amoroso, Will Hope-Ross, Jason Mehmel—these long lines of collaboration are a golden thread and mean the world.

Playwright's Note

When the idea came first to me many years ago, I did not know it would be a play. What I saw was an image: the green/blue arteries and tributaries of the Athabasca River, the watershed for the continent. Then came a picture of a pre-born child floating in the peaceful world of the womb. The river was the umbilical cord, all the rivers and streams the placenta. The images flickered, then became one. Gradually the characters (based in part on family, friends and loved ones) emerged, began speaking to me and disagreeing with one another and I knew I had to go where this play took me. I grew up in a fishing town in southwest Nova Scotia/the Mi'kma'ki, where, in the space of two generations, small-scale sustainable single boat fishers have been displaced by huge ocean draggers that tear up the sea bottom. We lost family to the sea as they ventured ever offshore to make a living. Many of us went overland west or north in search of work to sustain our families. Living first in the east and now in the west, I began to ask myself hard questions about extractive industries. Fish. Oil. How they connect through water. When I wrote the first notes for this piece, I hadn't yet children of my own; now I do, which brings the question of what we leave to the future even closer to home.

The hard edges of this play, I hope, are balanced by warmth, laughter and human connection, and in that I take my cue from my family and friends, many of whom work in these demanding environments and who have inspired this play.

Natalie Meisner
Summer 2025

Director's Note

When we premiered *Boom Baby*, we also hosted a round of short lectures by Mount Royal University academics. One of them said of Natalie's work that it has a spark to it, a spark that gives off light rather than heat. I loved hearing that, because it perfectly captured what it's like to work with Natalie, to be friends with her, to share a few minutes over coffee.

Natalie Meisner definitely has a spark... it animates her in ways that end up being contagious; you'll catch the spark as well.

Our friendship blossomed, in many ways, as sparks in recognition of each other.

This spark, this light to see by, is what takes both of us through the challenges of life. The spark: its light shows us the next steps in front of us, the small steps we can take as we try to move towards better realities.

Those better realities, full of kindness and care, full of hope, are a thread running through the stories Natalie writes, the poetry that she speaks, the laughter that she shares.

I won't explain the plot of *Boom Baby*; if you're reading this I expect you have at least a sense of it. But I will note that much of the play is in dialogue with the landscape around it, how affected it has been by the energy industry, and how depressing that can feel for a person who lives there. It would be easy to let those feelings scare away any possibility of hope.

At the core of all of it, a baby, and every question that it raises. Yet hope never fully disappears.

This is only one facet of the story, but I point it out because the moments of hope in *Boom Baby*, both large and small, are some of my most treasured memories from this production.

I feel very fortunate that my long-running collaboration with Natalie also allowed me to explore new sparks of hope among our fantastic and dedicated cast and crew.

That same spark lights Natalie's way through so many ideas and observations about the world she moves through; this is another thread in our friendship.

Directing *Boom Baby* was stepping inside the feelings and ideas that fill Natalie and I whenever we visit, informed by the entire village-sized family of collaborators that were part of the development of the script. I am excited that you get to share that spark as well.

Jason Mehmel

Jason Mehmel is the artistic director of SAGE Theatre. He directed the premiere of Boom Baby.

Foreword

Boom Baby is one of those works that gets under your skin. It crackles with witty dialogue and engaging characters, but underneath, the themes are substantive. It does not let you look away. It explores so many dichotomies—east and west, labourer vs management, poverty vs wealth, the tremendous need for resources vs the cost. Natalie Meisner looks through the lens from different angles, trying to ensure different perspectives are explored and recognizing there are never easy answers.

Natalie is a writer for whom I will always show up. Her work engages while challenging the audience to look outside themselves and their expectations or preconceived notions. She is interested in taking on the tough subjects and finding her way through them, exploring their relationship to her values and the challenges of the world in which we live. She does not shy away from them and has the exceptional gift of being able to approach them with humour as well as heart, making us laugh while we navigate sometimes difficult and painful realities.

When Natalie first gave me a draft of *Boom Baby* to read, it focussed quite heavily on Manley L. Natland, a petroleum geologist who had the idea to detonate a nuclear blast under Alberta making it easier to access the valuable resources beneath the ground by forcing them to the surface. The intense heat would take the thick tarry bitumen and convert it into liquid, which would be easier to extract. Though this idea is fascinating, and Manley L. Natland an interesting figure, he is not the heart of this story. His role was downgraded from a character to someone discussed as a theorist whose ideas still get resurrected by times.

What became very clear, as we worked on this piece over myriad workshops and readings with actors, is that the real heart of this story has always been Iona's unborn child. That baby, who we are not sure will even be born, depending on the decision Iona makes, represents so much. Babies by nature represent the future, but this baby, conceived so casually and unexpectedly in such a harsh climate, becomes a stand-in for our natural resources. For our potential. For our future, in a very tangible way. Who gets to control them? Who has a say? How will we manage them? Will we find a way to work together to protect them and keep them safe? Does it matter who "owns" them when we all stand to benefit from their care and growth?

The negotiation between Iona and Brooke, regarding who—if either of them—will keep the baby, was challenging to navigate. It reminded me of the two women in Berthold Brecht's *The Caucasian Chalk Circle* trying to prove who held the claim as the "true mother." Which one of them will do the right thing for the sake of the baby? But what is the right thing? What decision will create the best outcome? It is not always obvious (or what we have been conditioned to believe seems obvious may not really be true) and yet we strive to make meaningful and impactful decisions. Perhaps we need to search the unexplored roads to find the best route for the journey. Each character in *Boom Baby* has a very different preconceived idea—in hope or fear—of what is the best way forward. But the only way this child will be able to thrive is if they can put aside their own desires and ambitions and focus on what is best for this baby. The same can be said for this beautiful planet and the resources entrusted to us, as we navigate which paths to tread and whether they will create the best outcomes for the generations to follow.

Pamela Halstead
Summer 2025

Pamela Halstead is a director, dramaturge, actor, teacher, and arts administrator. She was the dramaturge for Boom Baby.

Production History

Boom Baby was first developed with Playwrights Atlantic Resource Centre (PARC) with dramaturge Pamela Halstead. It has had staged readings at Eastern Front Theatre, Handsome Alice, Alberta Theatre Projects, The Red Deer Players, and a workshop production at Alumnae Theatre's Fireworks Festival. It won the Canadian National Playwriting Award (Theatre BC) as well as the Grand Prize in the Alberta Playwriting Competition, presented by Alberta Playwrights Network in Association with Theatre Alberta.

The premiere of *Boom Baby,* a SAGE Theatre production with support from Mount Royal University, ran from February 28 to March 8, 2025, at the Pumphouse Theatre in Calgary with the following cast and team:

Cast

Iona: ....Kendra Hutchinson
Hort: ....John McIver
Brooke: .... Camille Pavlenko
Owen: ....David Sklar
Justin: ....Spencer Streichert

Creative Team

Playwright: .... Natalie Meisner
Director: ....Jason Mehmel
Set and Lighting Design: ....Brad Leavitt
Stage Manager & Lighting Design: .... K Hall

Associate Producer &
Assistant Director: ....Dylan Lindsay

Assistant Director: ....Madelaine Taylor-Gregg

Support Team

(For SAGE) Box Office Support: .... Sylviane Allard

(For MRU) Marketing and
Communication RA: .... Heather Seaba

Production RA: .... Morgan Laidley

Student Directed
Readings Team: ....Isra Abdulrahim,Becky Bona,
Spencer Heindle, Christina Jarmics,
Catherine Law, Victoria Mitchell

Editing: .... Dianne Richards

Three pals from the Maritimes explore their options in the oil sands. Iona (Kendra Hutchinson), Hort (John McIver), and Justin (Spencer Streichert) huddle around a campfire in an improvised campsite. Photo by Morgan Laidley.

Best friends Iona (Kendra Hutchinson) and Justin (Spencer Streichert) wake up "the morning after," and a discussion turns into a pillow fight. Photo by Morgan Laidley.

Brooke (Camille Pavlenko) and her husband Owen (David Sklar) discuss nuclear options in work and life. Photo by Morgan Laidley.

A marketing specialist for the oil sands, Brooke (Camille Pavlenko), lays out a company plan to return land to its natural state post-production in her video entitled *Blueprint for Tomorrow*. Photo by Morgan Laidley.

Iona (Kendra Hutchinson) and Hort (John McIver) discuss Iona's next steps as Hort has a drink. Photo by Morgan Laidley.

Company executives Owen (David Sklar) and Brooke (Camille Pavlenko) discuss surrogacy options with Iona (Kendra Hutchinson). Photo by Morgan Laidley.

Brooke (Camille Pavlenko) and Iona (Kendra Hutchinson) meet to discuss the possibility of surrogacy. Photo by Morgan Laidley.

Justin (Spencer Striechert) is alone with his thoughts. Photo by Morgan Laidley.

Character List

Iona: (20s) A heavy equipment operator from the East Coast.

Justin: (20s) A heavy equipment operator from the East Coast.

Hort: (20s, slightly older) a heavy equipment operator, Justin's friend, who grew up in the same small town.

Brooke: (Late 30s) A public relations specialist for mining companies in the Canadian North.

Owen: (Late 30s–early 40s) An engineer working for an extraction company. Married to Brooke.

Note: The team members in Act One, Scene 4 with Brooke can be played by other cast members in silhouette.

Setting

The camps, town, and surrounds of an enormous open pit mining operation.

Notes on Production

The scenes should run continuously until the act break. The set can be composed minimally and suggestively with items that might be found in a work camp environment. The young people are dressed for outdoor work and the older characters in upscale business casual.

Notes on the Text

Manley L. Natland was a real American geologist who, in 1956, proposed a radical way of accessing the oil buried deep under the sands: Why not nuke Alberta? An initial nine-kiloton atomic bomb, followed by others as large as one hundred kilotons, would be detonated underground, boiling the oil out of the sand and causing it to pool in caverns, where it could later be tapped conventionally.

The idea was shelved, but there have been recent attempts to revive the idea of nuclear power in Alberta, either to power electricity, or more recently, to power AI.

ACT ONE

Scene 1 *(quit eating tomatoes)*

An improvised camp/living site in the Canadian North. There are trucks, machinery, some clothes hanging up. RVs and campers and firepits. This is not camping for fun but camping by necessity. Three friends sit around one of the firepits. No one is singing campfire songs.

JUSTIN: I'm cold.

IONA: Cold is a state of mind.

JUSTIN: Cold in places I don't even want to talk about.

HORT: Oh, piss and moan.

IONA: Suck it up and pay rent like the rest of us.

JUSTIN: I don't know how much longer I can take this, Hort.

HORT: That kinda talk is completely destructive to the project at hand.

JUSTIN: Remind me, what is the project at hand?

HORT: We gotta talk about your pessimism, man. It has real effects in the world…it's quantum physics.

IONA: Oooh, quantum physics, fan-cy.

HORT: You create reality. You rearrange matter at the subatomic level every time you even look at something.

JUSTIN: *You* do, anyway. Your pa must rue the day he sent you off to school.

IONA: You didn't finish?

HORT: What's the point when you can make this kind of bank hauling dirt?

IONA: Listen, the pair of you need to just pay for bunks out at site. The last thing I need is to come out here and find the pair of you froze into your sleeping bags.

HORT: Sure, check into zombie central.

IONA: It's not that bad, actually.

HORT: Eat macaroni and tranquilizers and get fat.

JUSTIN: At least I'd be *warm* and fat.

IONA: You can buy your own groceries. No one is stopping you.

HORT: Enter serfdom. Be my guest, go consign your free will.

JUSTIN: Screw free will, I want to go home.

IONA: Nobody likes a quitter.

HORT: I am not pissing in a cup. Bust your ass all day, can't even have a nip of something to take the edge off. I ask you: is a man really a man if he's got to squat and piss like a bitch on demand?

IONA: I don't know, son, you tell me.

JUSTIN: Is your camp totally dry?

IONA: Officially. But you can get anything you want. Keta, coke, weed, of course—all varieties, and the beer flows like…wine.

JUSTIN: Really. Think you can get me in there?

IONA: *(Scans him.)* It's not like the bar is high.

HORT: That's a slippery slope. You picking up what I'm laying down here?

JUSTIN: You know…I'm not.

HORT: All those dudes. Shared showers.

IONA: Oh great, a homophobe!

HORT: No, no, man. Not me. If that's what floats your boat, you go get some. I won't judge.

JUSTIN: What in the blazes are you on about?

IONA: He's referring to your potential to get a prison wife. Actually, to *be* one, I guess…with your boyish good looks.

JUSTIN: *(To HORT.)* Fuck off, you two. *(To IONA.)* Wait—you think I'm good-looking?

IONA: *(Smacks his arm.)* Boyish, I said.

HORT: Once you're in there, they own you. They say when you eat, when you sleep.

IONA: I mean there *is* a schedule, if that's what you mean.

HORT: Yah, you're in the chick area. That's different. Special treatment.

IONA: Not special. All the trailers pretty much look the same.

JUSTIN: There's like a stench here, over the whole place. It coats the back of my throat. I can't get away from it.

HORT: No smoke, no baloney, like they say back home.

IONA: Sweet baby Jesus, for the love of all that's good and holy, do not get him started about back home!

HORT: Look, Justin, this campsite might not be the Hilton—

JUSTIN: You made it sound like El Dorado.

HORT: But we're lucky to have it.

JUSTIN: All you have to do is get a plane ticket, he says…

HORT: I got you a job the day you got here.

JUSTIN: I *know*, man.

IONA: Nothing back home gets you this kind of money. Nothing legal, anyway.

JUSTIN: Sure, but everything costs so much. The other day I just wanted a grilled cheese and tomato sandwich. Simple thing, right? I get up to the checkout and the tomatoes cost five dollars each!

IONA: Boo-hoo. Quit eating tomatoes. Or you could grow some yourself. You know, in a pot, on a window ledge.

JUSTIN: We live in a frigging camper! *(To HORT.)* You said we'd have a place.

HORT: *(Gestures grandly.)* This…is a place.

JUSTIN: A gravel pit with a leaky fifth wheel? We can't stay here all winter.

HORT: We'll find something.

JUSTIN: Where's the fucking milk and honey, man? You made it sound like the land of opportunity. Where's my doublewide trailer and my plasma TV, you skunk-headed freak?

HORT: *(To IONA.)* He's just pissed 'cause his girl back home isn't returning his texts.

IONA: Got a girl back home, do you?

HORT: He did. Out of sight, out of mind, till you get back home with the paycheque.

JUSTIN: Don't listen to him. Caroline's a good girl.

HORT: Sure, pard!

IONA: You can't call a grown woman a girl, Justin.

JUSTIN: Look out, she's about to go all flaming feminista on us.

IONA: *(Waves him off.)* You wish.

HORT: *(To JUSTIN.)* Fifty bucks says your "good girl" is boning someone down on the wharf right now.

IONA: *(To JUSTIN.)* Don't listen to him—he's a pig. *(To HORT.)* You're a pig.

HORT: That may well be, but at least this little piggy gets to market.

JUSTIN: Shut up, Hort. *(To IONA.)* He talks like that all the time and, it's amazing, but he still gets girls. Sorry…I mean…ladies? What do I say, what's the right word?

IONA: Women, you could try.

JUSTIN: Okay, women…even really pretty ones, to pay attention to him.

IONA: We hunks of firewood, however, are not feeling the charm.

JUSTIN: I didn't mean—Iona, I mean you are…

IONA: No need.

HORT: You can't be intimidated by a girl because she's hot. Not like she did anything to deserve it.

JUSTIN: Here he goes. God help us.

HORT: A pretty girl is nothing but an overly symmetrical freak of nature.

IONA: You're a great one to toss around the term "freak."

HORT: She gets used to counting on her looks. Well, it gives you an angle. Don't notice it. No, instead you find out what she's hiding, what she's running from. You find that, BAM! You're in.

IONA: Wow.

JUSTIN: That's messed up, man. You can't study women like bugs.

HORT: No? Ask me what the female praying mantis does to the male during the act. *(No one does, but no matter.)* Eats his head. Yeah, right at his weakest. Just as he's getting his rocks off? CHOMP! Nom, nom nom, she just eats his whole head.

JUSTIN: *(To IONA, waving at HORT.)* I'm sorry.

IONA: *(Waves it off.)* A year up here? Nothing offends me now.

HORT: See? Iona…She's different, she's one of us.

IONA: What's the right thing to say, here…? Thank you? Fuck you? I'm torn.

HORT: Besides, I have my doubts if she's even got a pussy hiding under all that Gor-Tex. Maybe, maybe not. Flash it, I'm willing to take a look.

IONA: Pass. *(Beat.)* Actually, let's have a look at yours first.

JUSTIN: Burn!

JUSTIN holds out his bottle, he and IONA clink.

HORT: *(To IONA.)* Yeah, you're all right. It's the rest that are venomous bitches.

IONA: I see. The rest of all women are venomous bitches.

HORT: Women in general, I love. Big, little, short, tall, I love them all. But here? Pit vipers, man. Won't even accept a drink from you until they know what you're pulling.

JUSTIN: *You* always want to know where a woman's working, first thing.

HORT: That's different, I have to make sure she's not a whore.

IONA throws her hands in the air. JUSTIN shakes his head.

HORT: I have standards.

JUSTIN: Standards? Son, you'd have a go at a rubber boot after you got a six pack in ya.

HORT: *(Pointing.)* Three o'clock. There's a fit bird one fire down. You know her? Where does she work?

JUSTIN: You're a complete hypocrite, you realize?

HORT: I do. You go by, make a pass and soften her up for me.

JUSTIN: I am not doing that.

HORT: You are lacking the necessary skills to survive in the wild. You'll excuse me, I got to drain the dragon. You two kids behave: Don't do anything I wouldn't do.

IONA: That rules out...what? Necrophilia and cannibalism?

HORT leaves.

JUSTIN: Sorry about that. He's...

Pause, JUSTIN thinks about it, isn't sure what to say.

IONA: Go on, I'm interested.

JUSTIN: A pain in the ass before he's in his cups...and homicidal right afterward. *(Beat.)* He's hard to make excuses for. *(Beat.)* He's got my back, though.

IONA: That's a thing. Especially up here.

JUSTIN: Yeah, but he's got that kind of "go for broke" gleam in his eyes. Don't know if I'm up for it tonight. You want to get a beer someplace?

IONA: Truth be told I wouldn't mind getting out of here.

JUSTIN: Should we hit the Rusty Bucket?

IONA: Ten o'clock. We'll run right into the Maritime ambush. End up in a headlock under some sweaty armpit shooting whiskey and singing "Barrett's Privateers."

JUSTIN: I'll keep 'em at bay.

IONA: All right, I mean it's fun and all but they're never happy till you puke.

JUSTIN: Let's go. I'll text Hort.

IONA: I'm game. He's onto Miss Three O'clock anyway.

They leave.

Scene 2 *(final solution)*

BROOKE and OWEN are in bed. She has a book open across her chest. He has a laptop on the side table.

OWEN: Babe, can you take a look-see at this proposal for me before lights out?

BROOKE: *(She reads.)* Nuclear? They'll never go for it.

OWEN: Who won't?

BROOKE: Let me see: the shareholders, the board, any environmental agency, the Sierra Club...

OWEN: The Sierra Club can talk to me when they quit burning up jet fuel to go to their international bitch sessions in Aspen.

BROOKE: Not to mention the peoples upon whose land we stand.

OWEN: The First Nations want this development. They leased us the land.

BROOKE: Indigenous peoples is the preferred term.

OWEN: Well, they change the damn term every six months.

BROOKE: So what if they do?

OWEN: It's frustrating! You have to do this dance of discomfort every time you start a conversation.

BROOKE: And your comfort is definitely the biggest dog in this fight.

OWEN: I get it. They have been repeatedly and historically wronged. That shit was bad and evil.

BROOKE: Is. Present day.

OWEN: I hear you, we're doing all the consults, don't worry. *(Beat.)* Just a quick peek, and tell me what you think.

Pushes laptop toward her. She takes it somewhat reluctantly, begins reading.

BROOKE: Nuclear runs counter to everything we're trying to do. We're transitioning to solar. We're remediating. We're pasturing bison on reclaimed sites…

OWEN: I know, I know. I love all that. This is not an either/or. This is and/and. Not one of those things alone is going to keep us all warm. Frankly, I don't even know if we'll ever get a shovel in the dirt on this one. Just help me finesse this enough to unlock those sweet research dollars.

BROOKE: *(Shakes her head; is this my life?)* How is it my job to finesse nuking the boreal forest?

OWEN: Not the whole thing, just this bit. *(Shows her on map.)* Look, we are going nuclear. It's not if, it's when. Nuclear is cleaner, you could say greener.

BROOKE: You can *say* it but—

OWEN: France already gets 70% of their power from nuclear.

BROOKE: Oui, mais ce n'est pas la France.

OWEN: Point Lepreau makes a quarter of New Brunswick's energy! No one there is screaming blue murder.

BROOKE: They did. No one listened.

OWEN: Okay, this is not a totally new idea. You know Project Cauldron?

BROOKE: *(Listening.)* I don't actually—

OWEN: We've known for over a hundred years that the oil was up here, but it's always been too costly to get at. This geologist in the '50s, Manley L. Natland, proposed a radical solution, one that might have just saved us all these tailing ponds, all this carbon.

He pauses a moment, wants her to ask.

BROOKE: What was it?

OWEN: Why not nuke Alberta?

BROOKE: Owen?

OWEN: Not the whole thing. Hear me out. A nine-kiloton nuclear device to start...lowered down a three-hundred-and-eighty-one-metre shaft...

BROOKE: *(Trying it out.)* Nine-kiloton nuclear device… Just rolls off the tongue.

OWEN: And bigger ones later, up to a hundred kilotons. You detonate them underground, pulverizing the rock and instantly boiling the oil out of it. POW. It pools in huge underground caverns. No waste materials, just several million cubic feet of freely flowing oil.

Pause. BROOKE sits up, examines him.

BROOKE: And why did our Mr. Natland not realize his dream, then?

OWEN: He worked for Richfield Oil, who, until very recently, held the patent to the process. This was not a blip; the idea really caught on. Hundreds of scientists—chemists, physicists, engineers, politicians, all working together to make this happen. The biggest fans? Albertans themselves.

BROOKE: *(What did you do?)* Wait. Until very recently, you said. What does that mean, exactly?

OWEN: Look, babe, we only made a small investment in the rights to the proprietary technology.

BROOKE: So this is like already a done deal? You did this…without telling me?

OWEN: There are so many irons in the fire, I can't run every one by you.

BROOKE: And who's *we*? The company?

OWEN: Not the whole company.

BROOKE: Who?

OWEN: Look, it's just a side deal. Brad and I saw an opportunity. If we can get the ear of the right people, we might be able to unlock some really big research funds, is all.

BROOKE: Fucking Bradley.

OWEN: No, it wasn't his idea. It was mine. The point is, we have a fear-based reaction to nuclear. It's not logical anymore. Reactors are not the giant death funnels from cartoons. The navy has them in submarines. They fit in the back of a pickup truck now, did you know that?

BROOKE: Back of a pickup. I did not know that and… I'm not sure how to feel about it. But no one is going to use nuclear explosions as a mining technique.

OWEN: Russia did.

BROOKE: Yeah, and who here remembers Chernobyl? Look, no one is going to let you detonate a land mass *(Looks at the map he is showing her on his computer.)* the size of New Brunswick to get the bitumen out of it.

OWEN: Are you sure? Zero emissions. Less waste than solar or wind turbines.

BROOKE: Do you have numbers to back that up?

OWEN: Yes!

BROOKE: What are you sucking me into?

OWEN: This is a hearts-and-minds play and if anyone can make it, it's you. It's closing time up here, unless we have a robust plan of action.

BROOKE: No, the only way forward is a consultative process with minimal impact on ancestral lands. That is in all my briefings.

OWEN: You know what's not in your briefings? Overseas investors have bailed, so we're holding the bag. It's adapt or die time. We need a big idea. A final solution.

BROOKE: Owen! You cannot say things like "final solution."

OWEN: *(He knows this, is playing contrarian.)* I can't?

BROOKE: Kind of a catchphrase for this unpopular guy from World War II.

OWEN: Honey, you know I slept through history class. That's what I have you for.

BROOKE: You are deliberately using inflammatory terms—

OWEN: I'm kidding. For Christ's sake!

BROOKE: You cannot let anybody on the board get wind of this. Nuclear payload is not going to buy us any goodwill at this point.

OWEN: Is this a board meeting? *(Looks around.)* I thought we were in bed. I thought I was spitballing ideas with my wife.

He tries to hand her a folder, she refuses.

BROOKE: Yes, but spinning our wheels on ideas—

OWEN: My hot, brilliant wife who thinks outside the box.

He caresses her playfully with the folder. She pretends not to notice.

BROOKE: No one is going to let you do this. Its batshit crazy.

OWEN: I have here bar graphs…a pie chart…I know how you love a good pie chart…

BROOKE: Stop. *(She enjoys it for a moment.)* Owen, something happened today. I kind of lost it for a minute.

OWEN: Yeah? Who caught your wrath?

BROOKE: You know that group that sits at the entrance to our office? In the nook near the foyer with the puppies and backpacks?

OWEN: I've been meaning to speak to security—

BROOKE: I'm not judging them, but—

OWEN: Don't judge, just keep paying their welfare cheques with your taxes.

BROOKE: Quit that!

OWEN: We can get those spikes on the ledges like they have at the bank—

BROOKE: No, that's not—that's awful! Okay, today they had a baby with them.

OWEN: A baby?

BROOKE: And I had an interaction with them that was not entirely positive...I guess you'd have to call it an altercation...

OWEN: You what?

BROOKE: This baby is still teething and they're feeding her candy. Her face is dirty, running with snot that no one bothers to wipe, and so I picked her up and—

OWEN: What?

BROOKE: Just to wipe off her face.

OWEN: Brooke? You can't do that.

BROOKE: And the girl got really upset. Screaming at me, "Give me back my baby!"

OWEN: Of course she did. In front of work?

BROOKE: Yes…

OWEN: What were you thinking? Did anyone see you?

BROOKE: No, it's fine. I put her down and backed away and they settled down. Everything is fine.

She puts her face into the pillow. Her body starts to shake as she cries silently.

OWEN: Aw, babe, don't. It's gonna be okay. There's that new procedure—

BROOKE: I'm tired. Of the procedures, the medications…

OWEN: You heard the doc; the advances in the field in the last ten years—

BROOKE: I did hear the doctor: "Your womb is an inhospitable environment." Just like this place. What are we even doing here?

OWEN: You love your job.

BROOKE: I make it work.

OWEN: How can you say that? You're the best we've got. Headhunters are always trying to scoop you up—

BROOKE: I apply myself. But with the assumption that we are going to be a family.

OWEN: *(Pause.)* I thought we were.

BROOKE: What?

OWEN: A family. Me and you and yes, eventually, children. But I've been operating under the assumption that we are already a family.

He moves toward her, sees she is not responding, drops his shoulders.

Scene 3 *(accept no substitutes)*

JUSTIN and IONA wake up in her bed, a mattress and box spring in the corner of her small room. Their clothes are in piles, and there is an empty 40 nearby. A low-wattage bulb on a small bedside table illuminates them slightly. She wakes up, turns over, and sees him.

IONA: Oh nooo. Did we? Fuuuuuck, noooo.

JUSTIN, groggy, looks around, gets his bearings. He's hungover but tries to be cheerful and gentlemanly.

JUSTIN: Good morning.

IONA: Jesus H. Christ on a very small cracker. What are you doing here?

She paws around on her bedside table until she finds a tube of aspirin. Shakes out a couple and chews them.

As if without thinking, she shakes out a couple of aspirin for JUSTIN and holds them out. He takes them and chews them thoughtfully.

JUSTIN: Well, I don't want to presume, but I think we, ah...

IONA: *(Gently taps her own skull.)* Stupid, stupid, stupid. *(Tries to put it together.)* We were having shots at The Bucket.

JUSTIN: Which I mean *(Beat.)* I'm a bit confused, 'cause Hort said you're not into guys.

IONA: 'Cause I'm not into him?

JUSTIN: Well, are you?

IONA: I…am just…not into labels.

JUSTIN: You like girls, then?

IONA: Yeah, maybe. I don't know, I'm working it out.

JUSTIN: Cool. That's cool.

IONA: No, it's not cool. You're my friend. It's… blech.

JUSTIN: Blech? Why is it blech? *(Sniffs his armpits.)* Do I reek?

IONA: Little bit of stale Axe body spray. You're all right.

JUSTIN: What then? Wasn't too bad, was I?

IONA: On a scale of one to ten? One being meh and ten being earth-shattering…

JUSTIN: That was the rum talking. Give me another chance; I'll pull up my socks.

IONA: It was fine. What I remember, anyway. You were fine.

Pause. He does not like the sound of that.

JUSTIN: Fine. Alrighty then.

IONA: Oh, don't go wounded stag on me. This is neither the time nor the place—

JUSTIN: Fine? Fine is what you say when you ask for a Coke and they bring Pepsi!

IONA: Don't be such a sook.

JUSTIN: I'm not a sook, you're a sook!

He hits her with a pillow.

IONA: Oh, that's real mature.

WHAM! Hits her again.

I'm warning you. Don't start something you can't finish.

JUSTIN: Bring it!

They have a huge pillow fight, held in check only by them still being hungover…Until JUSTIN finally relents.

All right, all right! Uncle.

She gets up, rummages in the cupboard.

IONA: We better eat something. I have some Shreddies. *(Brightens.)* Oh. Instant coffee. Do you take milk? Get up, put your pants on. No milk, but we have this milk-like stuff. *(Reads the label.)* International Delight. You want that in it?

He gets up, gets his jeans on kind of under the covers, looks a little lost.

Hello? Earth to Justin. You want this in there or not?

She holds up a bottle of artificial creamer.

JUSTIN: Sure, I guess.

IONA: What's the matter?

JUSTIN: It's just this is kind of a new feeling.

IONA: What do you mean, new? Sweet baby Jesus, don't tell me I've divested you of your virginity. There was some doubt in the local parish, but this seals it: I'm going to hell.

JUSTIN: Not like that. I mean, I've slept with girls.

IONA: "Slept with"—adorable. You mean Caroline?

JUSTIN: Other girls, too.

IONA: Sure, Mac.

JUSTIN: But it's usually…different.

IONA: Oh, can we just— *(Still rummaging, finding little.)* Friggin' bunkies! Scavengers! Have they got to eat every blessed crumb? Different how?

JUSTIN: Well, you don't just up and start a pillow fight.

IONA: Unless you're buds. Who should have stayed that way, but for that last round of shooters. I'm still tasting some nasty thing in the back of my throat…Was it fireball?

JUSTIN: I don't know if that's true…

IONA: What?

JUSTIN: That we need to stay just friends.

IONA: Oh, it is.

JUSTIN: Do you have to act like a jerk?

IONA: It's no act. This is me.

She comes back with a couple beers, a box of cereal, and a couple bowls for a hungover morning picnic.

So here's what we'll do. We'll avoid each other for a couple days, then meet up for beers and pretend like this never happened.

JUSTIN: Got it all worked out, have you?

Hands him bowls and beers.

IONA: Yes.

JUSTIN: Well, what if I don't want to?

His hands are full, she makes a grab and gets his phone. Flips through.

IONA: Here we go, where are you now? Sweeeet Caroline…

JUSTIN: Give me my phone.

IONA: BAH BAH BAH!

JUSTIN: Give it!

IONA: Justin, if you're gonna go whore-dogging around, at least better put a lock on your phone. Oh, found her. The redhead.

JUSTIN: Give it.

She knows the room better than him, dodges. She finds a really nice picture of Caroline, looking right at the camera. Stops clowning.

IONA: She's pretty. Looks smart, too.

JUSTIN: She is.

IONA: What does she do?

JUSTIN: Works at the old folks' home. Saving up for a nursing degree.

IONA: Asshole! *(Punches him in the arm.)*

JUSTIN: What? You knew about her.

IONA: I knew *of* her, as a nameless abstraction. Now that I have a clear picture, it's different. Shut up and eat your Shreddies.

JUSTIN grabs his phone back. Mopes.

She looks at him.

C'mon. Stop being weird.

JUSTIN: But you're just acting like last night was nothing and—

IONA: Look, this was stupid, but I don't have a lot of friends up here. Or anywhere, really. I can't really stand to lose one. So how about this: We don't have to avoid each other, we just say fuck it, and start being normal right now? Okay? Go.

JUSTIN: What? I don't know what to say.

IONA: Tell me some more about that house you're gonna build.

JUSTIN: It's a house. So what? What's there to say?

IONA: *(Prompting him.)* Couldn't shut up about it last night. The thickness of the walls, the grade of the driveway.

JUSTIN: You do have to get the right slope on it, from the get-go. *(Beat.)* Pipe dream, anyway. Can't save any money up here. Everything here costs an arm and a leg. Food, gas, beer. You get your cheque and it just goes.

IONA: I hear ya.

JUSTIN: What you saving up for?

IONA: I have family who…My mother needs help… you know how it is.

JUSTIN: Sure enough. What about after that?

IONA: Well, then I want to get out there and see some of the world.

JUSTIN: Oh yeah, what do you want to see, Iona Macpherson?

IONA: I don't know—pyramids! The desert, the jungle: *National Geographic* stuff. Real cities that have as many people in them as this whole frozen-ass country.

JUSTIN: That sounds pretty good.

IONA: Toss my belongings in a backpack and I'm gone, son.

JUSTIN: Doing your time. Like me. But for the time being, anyway, here we are. I suppose that's why…

Pause. JUSTIN is looking down at his phone at the picture of Caroline.

IONA: Look, don't beat yourself up too hard. *(Beat)* You were thinking about her the whole time we were fucking.

JUSTIN: I was not.

IONA: Were too.

JUSTIN: No—

IONA: It's okay. I was doing it too. We all create substitutes…

JUSTIN: Who? Who were you thinking about?

IONA: No way, forget it.

JUSTIN: It's like that commercial—accept no substitutes…

IONA: That's life up here.

JUSTIN: You want tomatoes but you settle for ketchup.

IONA: *(Holds up the stuff for his coffee.)* You want cream in your coffee, but you get some gross white oil called "International Delight."

JUSTIN: When you think about it, guess we're accepting substitutes for…just about everything.

Pause. IONA takes this in.

IONA: Don't take this the wrong way, but you don't seem like the type to come up here. Hort talk you into it?

JUSTIN: He bailed me out, actually. I spent the eight months before I got here laying on the couch. *(Shakes his head.)* Ah, can't get into all that.

IONA: What? Come on, Justin.

JUSTIN: I'm meant to be fishing at this time of the year, but…ah…season before last, Dad and his crew were trying to get the last set of traps in before closure. They were pushing it, you know, but that's nothing new. Anyways, they lost some power in the engine, couldn't stay ahead of the storm. And the boat, she…

He breaks off, he can't speak.

IONA: Where'd it go down?

JUSTIN: George's Bank.

IONA: Oh, no. I'm sorry.

JUSTIN: Dad, Uncle Lyon, Cousin Ren. *(Tries to pull himself together, takes a glug of beer.)* Wasn't for a bout of pneumonia, I'd be with them. Maybe better off, too.

IONA: Don't say that.

Puts a hand on his shoulder for a minute—a comrade's touch.

JUSTIN: Promised Ma I'd never step a foot off the wharf again. But truth be told, even after all that's happened, I'd still rather be out on the water than here.

IONA: The sea gets in your blood.

JUSTIN: That she does. Gets in your blood like lead poison when she takes the ones you love.

They clink bottles, a sad, knowing toast.

Scene 4 *(toads to speak of)*

BROOKE is chairing a communications meeting. We can hear but not see a couple of members of her team in the semidarkness as she flicks through slides of bucolic woodland scenes: rows of neatly planted trees, pristine pools of water.

BROOKE: Okay, I think we have everyone. If we stay on track here, maybe we can wrap before lunch.

As ever, sustainability and responsible stewardship are top of mind. The public still aren't aware that land can be returned to its natural state post-production. So, we need to run with simple, powerful landscape images with narration, "We have planted over five million trees on reclaimed land and are investing five hundred million dollars in renewables." Can we get someone with a distinctive voice, like a public figure?

TEAM MEMBER 1: Yeah, that might be hard…

BROOKE: Okay, some company people, even better. I could do it: "I want to stand out here and fish with my sons one day." That kind of thing.

TEAM MEMBER 2: I didn't know you have kids.

BROOKE: *(She smiles, annoyed.)* I don't. It was a figure of speech.

TEAM MEMBER 1: Didn't really take you for the fishing type.

BROOKE: Okay, okay, I hear you. We keep it factual, direct. Music and stats across the bottom of the screen. "One-point-six billion dollars invested in air quality. Eighty-five percent of the water we use is recycled." And...did you all know this? We are the first company in history to actually construct a fen out of a reclaimed mining site.

TEAM MEMBER 1: Fen. What's a fen?

BROOKE: A fen is a crucial part of the boreal forest ecosystem. It is a wetland fed by surface and groundwater.

TEAM MEMBER 2: Like a bog. For the ducks to swim.

BROOKE: Not a bog, a *fen*. A fen provides habitat for peat moss.

TEAM MEMBER 1: Majestic animals. Can we get some elk in there? Snout toward the camera, dripping muzzle…you know, drinking—

BROOKE: Elk do not frequent fens.

TEAM MEMBER 1: How about bears?

BROOKE: No, the water in a fen is high in naphthenic acids—those are naturally occurring, by the way, but large animals don't tend to… Look, fens are great for the growing of peat moss.

TEAM MEMBER 2: *(Unenthusiastic.)* Peat moss. Can we film that?

BROOKE: Peat moss, you might be interested to know, has been indispensable to generations of Indigenous people due to its insulating and absorptive qualities. They used it as a natural refrigerator, biodegradable diapers, mattress stuffing—

TEAM MEMBER 1: Does a fen have any frogs?

BROOKE: No.

TEAM MEMBER 2: Toads to speak of?

TEAM MEMBER 3: Come on, you guys, cut her some slack.

BROOKE: No.

TEAM MEMBER 1: Insects…minnows…?

BROOKE: No, no.

TEAM MEMBER 2: So, ducks would be out of the question…?

BROOKE: THERE ARE NO FUCKING DUCKS IN A FEN, OKAY? IF EVERYONE WAS AS CONCERNED WITH HUMAN BEINGS AS THEY WERE WITH DUCKS WE'D HAVE WORLD PEACE AND BROTHERLY LOVE, WOULDN'T WE?

There is a bit of a murmur from the team members. Some turn off their cameras. BROOKE puts her head down, composes herself.

You will have to pardon that… Fuck me, I'm sorry, you guys. Let's take a break. We all meet back in here in twenty with some fresh ideas, okay?

She powers off the slides, lights fade.

Scene 5 *(the humane thing)*

HORT and IONA are at the campsite. There is a big steel pot nearby. JUSTIN enters with a bag of lobsters.

JUSTIN: Two lobsters each! Put a pot on to boil, it's party time, fuckers!

IONA: Six? Must have cost you a fortune.

HORT: *(Rubs belly.)* Oh, yummm. Come to Papa. It's been so long.

IONA: Put them to sleep before you throw them in. You know the trick where you stand them on their heads?

HORT: I know the trick where I send them down me gullet.

IONA: You make a tripod with the claws and head. Stroke their backs for a minute and they pass out and never feel a thing.

JUSTIN: Lobsters don't feel anything. Tiny little brains.

HORT: Knife between the eyes, that's the humane thing to do. That's how I want to go if it's ever necessary, just so you two know.

JUSTIN: On the boat, we microwave them in a plastic bag. Cook in their own juices…No word of a lie, it's the best lobster you'll ever have. Little melted butter and vinegar… *(Digging in the cooler.)*

IONA: Needlessly cruel.

JUSTIN: What's cruel is the price. If we could get a quarter of that on the wharf…

HORT: Lobsters share a common ancestor with cockroaches.

JUSTIN: *(Digging in cooler.)* Where is the butter? Ah…

HORT: You know they call them the undertakers of the sea.

JUSTIN: *(Still digging, but not finding.)* White vinegar… where's the vinegar? *(Jabs a finger at HORT.)* You said we had vinegar.

HORT: Lobsters go for the tender parts first...the eye sockets, the flesh under the nails...the scrotum...

IONA holds her stomach, looks queasy.

JUSTIN: He's trying to gross you out so there's more for him. *(Rummaging, not finding it.)* Don't tell me I have to go begging around the campsite for vinegar.

IONA: Never mind, we'll just eat it like this.

JUSTIN: No, no. I am going to get a decent meal if it's the last thing I do.

He heads over to another campsite.

HORT: Well, I'm not waiting. Let's dig in.

IONA does not. HORT notices.

Hungover? You hit it hard last night, didn't you?

IONA: No.

HORT: If you have the flu, you get up out of here right now. *(Making a warding off, a hex sign.)* I can't afford a bunk day.

IONA: It's not the flu.

IONA grabs a bucket nearby and leans over it; for a second it looks like she might puke, but it passes.

HORT: What then? You're green around the gills. Didn't know better I'd think you were knocked up or something.

She sits down, drops her head into her hands.

What? You can't be pregnant.

IONA: I know that. Shh!

HORT: Not up here! Wait, you don't even do dudes! Or do you?

IONA: Not usually…Can you just—

HORT: Why is no one telling me anything around here? Whose is it?

IONA looks to see if JUSTIN is coming back.

IONA: Shut your mouth, Hort.

HORT: Justin? WHAT? You two are knocking boots behind my back?

IONA: It was just one time. We were hammered—

HORT: Shiiit. Are you sure?

IONA: A whole box of tests. They all came out positive.

HORT: Ohhh. And you haven't told him.

IONA: No, I'm not going to.

HORT: Come again?

IONA: My own fucking fault. I'll take care of it. He doesn't want anything to do with a baby.

HORT: Of course not. Actually, hold on. You know what? I take that back. Suddenly I can totally picture that guy with a couple of ankle-biters. His ma would be fucking tickled pink. Hey, maybe he does. Why don't you ask him?

IONA: *I* don't.

HORT: You don't. Now that's different. How far in?

IONA: About six weeks.

HORT: Daaamn. You gotta tell him.

IONA: No. And you can't either. You know him, he'll have all kinds of feelings about it and I can't…just forget I said anything.

HORT: No, I mean seriously. *(Low whistle.)* You can't go out to site with a bun in the oven; it's dangerous out there.

IONA: I know that.

HORT: Dude, you are totally screwed. I would not want to be in your shoes right now.

IONA: Thanks, asshole.

HORT: Go to the doc?

IONA: Eight hours at the walk-in clinic, and what for? For them to tell me what I already know? I just feel so…

She winces, puts her hands on her own legs, her stomach.

…hijacked! If I think about something, like, growing, taking root inside of me, I can't even…ugh!

HORT: You going to get rid of it?

IONA: I have to.

HORT: Need a drive?

IONA: You gonna drive me seven hundred and fifty clicks?

HORT: If I can get Justin's truck.

IONA: Add pulling over to puke, that's going to cost you two days' pay. You don't even know me.

HORT: I know you enough. There's a lotta people with a lot of strong feelings on this matter—

IONA: No shit.

HORT: But I am not one. I personally do not have any skin in this game. Your body, I say you get to decide about any little squidlets that you do or do not squirt out of it. *(Beat.)* I drove a girl last fall.

IONA: You did? Was it…yours?

HORT: No…I don't think so, anyway. But she was a bit far along, which made the whole thing… worse, I would say. Afterward she needed to talk. She was a bit fucked up. So was I, by the time we got back, truth be told.

IONA: Oh, god.

HORT: Sorry, bud. Not trying to spook you.

IONA: No, I hear you. It's shit or get off the pot.

HORT: She made the hardest call I've ever seen anyone make. I drove her there, but she had to go in by herself. When she was done, they kept her for a little bit, then we got some stale burgers and flat Cokes and drove back. But know what? She's happy now. She's kicking ass. Stuck to her life plan and that was the right call…for her.

IONA: *(Nods.)* Like, I know I don't want it in there, but if I think about taking it out…it makes me feel sick…

HORT: *(He nods, pauses.)* That a church thing?

IONA: No, I wasn't raised in the church. It's just... weird 'cause where I come from, it's babies having babies, and if my own mother had any options, I might not even be walking this earth, you know?

HORT: Whoa, that is some heavy shit.

IONA: I just started to get my ducks in a row. I didn't expect to have to make a life-or-death call before next rotation. Could you go Tuesday?

HORT: I can do that.

IONA: I'll buy the gas.

Pause as he takes it all in.

HORT: Okay. You want like a hug, or—

IONA: No. *(Beat.)* Just promise not to tell Justin. I do not need him gumming up the works.

HORT: I get it, but he's your friend, too.

IONA: Hort. You keep your mouth shut, or so help me god—

Almost by reflex he holds the bottle up to pass it.

HORT: You'll kill me. All right, I get it. Might as well have a smash, then.

She waves it off, still queasy, the bonfire flickers.

Scene 6 *(there is no we)*

JUSTIN has tracked IONA down working at the bar, he comes in and plunks down.

JUSTIN: You don't answer my messages now. What the hell?

IONA: I'm working!

JUSTIN: Eighteen texts, you can't answer one?

IONA: Well, fuck off with your eighteen texts, then. You're being weird—

JUSTIN: All that time waiting for rock to load and you did not have one minute last week to squeeze out an emoji? Who's being weird?

Pause. She looks at him. Shit, he knows.

IONA: Hort told you.

JUSTIN: He's my best friend. What did you think?

IONA: Prick.

JUSTIN: At least someone had the common decency to tell me I'm gonna be a father!

IONA: You're not. And don't go making this about you.

JUSTIN: How is it not about me? You get pregnant on your own?

IONA: Justin—

JUSTIN: I know we're not, like, a real couple, but I still—

IONA: Real? We're not any kind of a couple.

JUSTIN: But that doesn't mean you can screw me over like this.

IONA: You? I'm the one who'll get shit-canned from work!

JUSTIN: Why did you tell Hort, and not me?

IONA: I didn't mean to, and I knew you'd freak the fuck out, just like you're doing.

He takes that in. It stings, but…

JUSTIN: Be that as it may, don't you think I'm in my rights to know?

IONA: Well, fine, Mr. Precious Rights. So now you know, you're in the shitter too. Happy?

JUSTIN: Iona, listen to me, right now. I know you're scared.

IONA: I am *not* scared—

JUSTIN: A million things must be going through your mind…but let's slow down and think this through.

IONA: I don't have time, Justin.

JUSTIN: Okay, okay. I understand. I mean, I…put a rubber on, didn't I?

IONA: I honestly can't—I don't remember everything.

JUSTIN: I'm so sorry, I really thought I did, honestly, Iona.

IONA: It's not your fault.

JUSTIN: I want you to know I accept the responsibility. I am not one to run away on you.

IONA: Please don't—

JUSTIN: Now, this is a hard old place to have a baby, for sure…

IONA: Don't say "baby," it's not—

JUSTIN: Just, please, Iona, you can't.

IONA: You think I can keep it? What am I gonna do? Change diapers on the dashboard of the digger? Got a real nice daycare out at site, do they?

JUSTIN: I said I'll help you.

IONA: I don't want your help.

JUSTIN: Please, you cannot kill the baby.

He tries to gently reach for her, she is not having that.

IONA: Don't fucking touch me!

JUSTIN: We'd never be able to live with ourselves.

IONA: STOP! Talking…Right now.

But he can't stop. She drops her head into her hands for a moment to retain some calm.

JUSTIN: You would do that to an innocent little baby that never hurt a soul… *(Breaks off, horrified.)*

IONA: It's my body. If I decide to end the pregnancy, it's my decision.

JUSTIN: I can't let you do this.

IONA: You don't have a say in it. Besides, I'm doing you a favour.

JUSTIN: For frig sakes, Iona. How is this a favour? Maybe things aren't perfect, but for whatever reason—I was there—we made a life together.

IONA: Stop saying *we*. There is no *we*, dumbass.

JUSTIN: I swear, if you call me a name one more time—

IONA: Why? What are you going to do, dumbass? Hit me?

She gets in his face. He is upset but does not move.

Go on, I'll smash you right back. It'll be good to feel something besides this stuck, numb feeling.

JUSTIN: I'm not gonna hit a woman.

IONA: Of course you're not.

JUSTIN: A pregnant woman, no less. The mother of my child.

IONA: Jesus wept. Don't call me, okay? Don't text. Leave me alone.

JUSTIN: You can't do this.

IONA: Fuck off.

She walks away from him and heads out back.

Scene 7 *(outside the box)*

BROOKE and OWEN are in bed. He is mumbling in his sleep, and she nudges him.

OWEN: Wha—Oh, sorry, honey. Was I snoring?

BROOKE: Mumbling. Protons, neutrons. Something, something. I couldn't quite make it out. But now that we're up…

OWEN: Are we?

BROOKE: I need to talk to you about something.

OWEN: Now? *(Beat, she does not respond.)* Okay, now.

He reaches onto his bedside table, turns on a light.

So now that we're up at 3:30 a.m., what is it?

BROOKE: I have been thinking about our current dilemma. And this is maybe not a conventional solution, but it could really be great.

OWEN: What could be really great?

BROOKE: You are always telling me, "divergent thinking," right? Get outside the box; that's where all the good ideas are…

OWEN: What box? Brooke? You're not making sense.

BROOKE: Well, I am doing that. I may have found someone to help us have a baby.

OWEN: What do you mean? Like a surrogate?

BROOKE: Yeah, like that.

OWEN: But we haven't even talked about this.

BROOKE: You *won't* talk about it.

OWEN: That's not true—but this is a new direction. I mean, we'd have to get an egg from you, a sperm from me, go to an agency…it's a whole process. Then we'll have to find the right person.

BROOKE: It's a lot, right? It can take years.

OWEN: Right. I mean, we can discuss it, but I don't think we need to be up at this hour—

BROOKE: I mean, here we are, tying ourselves in knots trying to conceive, undertaking some onerous process. But what if…there was already someone right here? Right under our noses.

OWEN: Look, I'm half asleep. Can we just put a pin in this and—

BROOKE: No. So I was talking to some of the gang at work about our situation—

OWEN: Brooke! That's our personal business.

BROOKE: Just the broad strokes. Stephanie in HR knows a young woman at the Otter Creek site who's pregnant.

OWEN: Wait, whoa.

BROOKE: I mean, it makes so much sense, if you think about it. A young woman finds herself with a baby she can't keep and here we are—wanting a baby.

He sits upright. Scrambles for glasses.

OWEN: Brooke! She's already pregnant!?

BROOKE: Yes, that's what I am saying. We have to act fast.

OWEN: Are you out of your mind? Who is this person?

BROOKE: She's one of ours. Loader operator—

OWEN: What are you even proposing?

BROOKE: Well, I don't know…We'll find out. We'll have to get to know her.

OWEN: This is crazy talk. Just because person A has a baby, and couple B want a baby, it doesn't mean we can just take it off her hands.

BROOKE: Why not?

OWEN: People are going to ask questions.

BROOKE: I'll answer the questions. That's what I do.

OWEN: A worker? You can't seriously be considering...I mean, she's probably been living the life.

BROOKE: Meaning?

OWEN: What if she's drinking? Using? I mean, they all are, pretty much. What are the chances the baby will be born healthy?

BROOKE: If our baby is sick, we'll love our baby and help our baby get better.

OWEN: Stop saying "our baby"—

BROOKE: So, if I get sick right now are you going to be, like, "Oh, bad deal. Take this back, it's broken"?

OWEN: Of course not. You're my wife. I know you—I love you. I don't know this girl, this baby, this fetus—or this zygote, I should say—

BROOKE: Don't be callous.

OWEN: How did you even find this person?

BROOKE: I told you. Stephanie.

OWEN: But we don't know a damn thing about this girl.

BROOKE: We'll find out on Friday.

OWEN: Friday?

BROOKE: When we meet her.

OWEN: What? No!

BROOKE: Yes. I told you this is a window of opportunity; we have to jump on it.

OWEN: We haven't even discussed this.

BROOKE: We're discussing. We're discussing right now.

OWEN: Let's say, for the sake of argument…we go to meet this person.

BROOKE: Great.

OWEN: Just ask yourself one thing: Are you sure you can trust yourself to be objective? Because on this topic…when it comes to babies, women just seem to go a bit crazy.

BROOKE: Right. That's what we do. "Go crazy." That's what you call the desire to nurture and love and be a part of the next generation. Of course, you all do that and it's oh so dignified, but a woman does it…

OWEN: No—

BROOKE: And it's: "Oh, she's hysterical. Someone get the straitjacket and the Prozac."

OWEN: Brooke, I want kids too, but don't you think you need to consult with me before you introduce this potential element of chaos into our life? *(Beat, more gently.)* There are so many advancements in the field, we've barely scratched the surface—

BROOKE: The treatments are destroying my body—

OWEN: Don't say that—

BROOKE: And, more importantly, they are not going to work.

Silence.

OWEN: You don't know that.

BROOKE: I do. *(Beat.)* Are you...worried you couldn't fully love a child that's not your blood?

OWEN: No, of course I could love...I mean, I want, obviously...to see you and me in our baby. I mean, your smile...on a tiny little face. Everyone wants that, don't they? Does that make me a monster?

BROOKE: No. But what if we can't have that? Then what?

OWEN: *If* we've exhausted all the possibilities...we'll do what normal people do. We'll adopt the legal way.

BROOKE: That takes years.

OWEN: We'll go overseas. There are kids all over the world who need parents.

BROOKE: But that makes no sense. Why go looking elsewhere when we have—right here in front of us—someone who needs love?

OWEN: Okay, let's look at this thing logically. So this girl wants to give up her baby for adoption.

(BROOKE nods.)

Because she's in a jam.

BROOKE: Right—it's a win-win.

OWEN: People are very volatile when their backs are against the wall.

BROOKE: You're preaching to the choir, my love.

OWEN: No, I mean—what I'm saying is that she might have the best of intentions now. But what if we make all these plans, become *invested,* and then she changes her mind and keeps it?

BROOKE: Stop saying "it."

OWEN: Fine. Keeps the baby. The baby in question who does not belong to us.

BROOKE: Not yet.

She reaches across him, turns off the bedside light.

Scene 8 *(blueprint for tomorrow)*

Early afternoon at the Rusty Bucket. It is nearly empty. IONA is behind the bar. BROOKE enters, looking around, and not seeing anyone else, she approaches the bar.

IONA: Cuba libre?

BROOKE: Bit early in the day for me. How'd you guess?

IONA: Fancy name for a rum and Coke. What can I get you?

BROOKE: *(Smiles, appreciating.)* Soda with a lime twist would be great. So, you must be Iona.

IONA: I suppose I must be, but right now I wish I had a choice. You management?

BROOKE: Communications.

IONA: How's *that* for work up here?

BROOKE: A challenge, for sure. Maybe you've seen *Blueprint for Tomorrow.*

IONA: Yeah, they make us watch it. In training.

BROOKE: You're one of ours, Stephanie said.

IONA: You got me. Yeah, loader operator. I just pick up the odd shift here on days off.

BROOKE: *(With interest.)* Having more women in the field is really important to the company.

IONA: Is it?

BROOKE: Tell me, the working conditions for you at site, how are they really?

IONA: The air exchange works. I have my own shitter, which is pretty coveted.

BROOKE: Are the men respectful toward you, as a woman?

IONA: "Woman," ha. You hear a million words for female out there, but you never hear that one.

BROOKE: I see.

IONA: You can't let them get under your skin—they feed on that.

BROOKE: That is a great read.

Pause. They take each other in. BROOKE looks at IONA with keen interest, as you would someone who might have a baby for you. IONA does not squirm but is not thrilled with the gaze.

IONA: Well, this is…weird.

BROOKE: I'm Brooke.

IONA: I know, you texted me.

BROOKE: Right. Should we sit here at the table? Or wait, I'll join you at the bar. I just want to start by thanking you so much for considering us for this exciting opportunity. And I want you to know that if we are your chosen adoptive parents, the child would—

IONA: Exciting? Opportunity? *(Blows through her lips or lets out a sigh.)* Words, words, words.

BROOKE: *(Checks herself.)* This must be a very challenging time for you.

IONA: You could say that. *(Looks around.)* Where's your—I thought you were married.

BROOKE: He's got to be on the way. One sec.

Boop. She texts. No response.

Let's…take this time to get to know each other a little bit.

IONA scrutinizes her. Her hands, her nails are done.

IONA: Nice French tips.

BROOKE: Thanks…

Weird; IONA does not seem like the type to give a rat's ass about manicures.

IONA: Took a course back home. Can't make any money at it.

BROOKE: *(Nods.)* It's a silly…indulgence, I know.

IONA: The chemicals they put in there…The fumes are like to choke you.

This has honestly not occurred to BROOKE before, but she considers it now.

BROOKE: Yes, if you breathe it in all day…

IONA: Plus, god, so boring. One week and I'm, like, "Just kill me now."

BROOKE: I can imagine.

She wants to engage IONA, but uncharacteristically she is at a loss for words.

IONA: You nervous?

BROOKE: *(Relieved to admit it.)* I am, actually, yes. *(Beat.)* Are you?

IONA: Yeah. I mean I just started to feel like I got my ducks in a row. And then this. It's like: Ducks? What are ducks?

BROOKE: Even considering bringing another life into this world…Everything else kind of seems puny in comparison.

IONA: Yeah…

BROOKE: How are you feeling? Are you nauseous?

IONA: *(Nods.)* Threw up a bit in my mouth just now because someone left sour cream and onion chips over there, and the smell—ugh.

BROOKE: *(Nods.)* Yeah, I found ginger tea helped. *(Looks hopefully behind bar.)*

IONA: *(Somewhat amused.)* I really doubt we'll find ginger tea back here.

BROOKE: *(Taking in the bar.)* Right.

IONA closes her eyes for a moment.

IONA: *(To herself.)* Jesus.

BROOKE is concerned.

BROOKE: Do you want to put your feet up? That helps sometimes. Have you felt any movement? Can I…?

BROOKE begins to reach out to touch IONA's belly, IONA raises her hand.

IONA: Please don't!

BROOKE: Sorry. As soon as you're pregnant everyone thinks your belly is public property. I know better than that.

They look into one another's eyes for a long moment.

I want you to know that Owen and I—if you decide to move forward with us—would be committed to preserving your autonomy at every turn.

IONA: My what?

BROOKE: This is entirely your decision. We don't want you to feel pressured in any way.

IONA: That's nice of you to say, but I have to decide by Tuesday.

BROOKE: Right.

IONA: I should probably just get rid of it.

BROOKE leans in, engaging IONA.

BROOKE: I totally support you, if you decide to terminate. But *if* you would consider adopting the child to us, I want you to know that my husband and I will support you in every aspect of this pregnancy.

IONA: What does that mean?

BROOKE: We can be a support network for you—

IONA: I take care of myself.

BROOKE: I can see that.

IONA grabs a non-alcoholic beer from a shelf behind her. BROOKE thinks it is a real one.

Maybe you shouldn't—

IONA: People in Europe drink beer for breakfast. Or so I've heard.

Takes a long swallow.

It's alcohol-free. I'm not an idiot.

BROOKE: Of course. I didn't mean…

IONA: I shouldn't have texted you. I don't know what I'm doing. I'm wasting your time.

BROOKE: Not at all. *(Regroups, takes a deep breath.)* It might be helpful to give you a bit more information about us. We came up here…let me think…going on ten years now.

IONA: So when are you leaving?

BROOKE: I don't know that we are. We came here for work, but now we're involved. The community garden, the greenspace plan...

IONA: How's that going for you?

BROOKE: Media wants to tell you it's all strip clubs and bar fights. Makes good copy. But you and I know it's not the reality.

IONA: Do we? Look around you. We are in the asshole of the universe.

BROOKE: The land has a rugged beauty.

IONA: Like the moon. *(Beat.)* Which is what this whole place is going to look like by the time we're all done up here. Which reminds me, I gotta be at site by 7 p.m.

IONA gathers up her things, preparing to leave. Damn, BROOKE's losing her...

BROOKE: A couple quick things about us. We have been trying to have a baby for such a long time and if you decide to carry and *if* you decide we might be the chosen parents, we would be so grateful.

IONA: Thanks, I have your contact info.

BROOKE: We've exhausted the alternatives in terms of having our own. We were able to conceive several times, but every time...

IONA: *(Turning to look at BROOKE.)* You lost them?

BROOKE: I gave each one a name...I felt it was important—

IONA: *(Holds up her hand.)* No, I can't. *(Beat.)* Brooke, I have one question for you.

BROOKE: Anything.

IONA: Are you or are you not a nut job?

BROOKE: On this particular topic—Look, Iona, I'm running out of time, too. If I am going to be a mother, I have to do it soon.

IONA: If this was as easy as donating blood, I would. But do you expect me to…about tear myself in half?

BROOKE: No, birth is a natural process. It can be beautiful!

IONA: I have seen the videos; your vagina is never the same again. You think I should go through all that, just to hand a kid over to a bunch of psychos to mess up?

BROOKE, listening carefully, disregards "psychos" and hears the underlying message.

BROOKE: That sounds like you might be…Are you… considering us?

IONA: *(Nods.)* Of the choices I have, which are pretty slim.

A surge of happiness comes over BROOKE; she tries to quell it.

BROOKE: Do you have any idea what just this chance… We would love and cherish— We would, of course, compensate you. You won't have to work while you're carrying the baby. You make something like this, I think?

BROOKE does a quick tally on a napkin, slides it over to Iona.

On a 12/8 split for eight. Plus rent and good food, of course. Does this sound about right?

IONA: You want to pay me this much…for a baby?

IONA backs away.

BROOKE: Pay? No, this is just housing costs…expenses and compensation for lost wages.

IONA: Man alive, you people can make anything seem clean.

End of Act I

ACT TWO

Scene 1 *(the old shell game)*

OWEN and BROOKE are in bed. There are books lying open on their spines, he balances a computer on his lap.

OWEN: So where the old CANDU nuclear reactors use heavy water, the new ones use organic coolant. Waste product is marginal. A drop in the bucket compared to any other extraction method. Brooke?

He looks something up on the computer, makes a note. BROOKE is not engaged but he has not noticed yet.

BROOKE: Drop in the bucket. Heard you.

OWEN: All the meltdowns like Chernobyl and Three Mile Island were fusion. The new ones are designed to shut down immediately in the event of a meltdown. People get all uptight over explosions, never thinking about the fact that combustion happens inside any engine every time they start it. Your pickup, your smart car, your goddamn lawnmower, any engine you start up is a controlled explosion. *(Beat.)* This happens with every innovation; we move through fear, to hubris, to finally being able to use it safely and practically... Brooke?

BROOKE: What is it?

OWEN: I was explaining something about the project…

BROOKE: So?

OWEN: So you're like a million miles away.

BROOKE: Look, Owen, I don't care. You want to nuke the whole place, go for it.

OWEN: Nuke it, no. We're looking at all kinds of options for next gen renewables too… You know that. Even if we do use this one, there'll be no big blast, just slow-burning tiny depth charges powered by thermonuclear… *(Realizes she is actively ignoring his work talk.)* Hello?

BROOKE: A half hour of your time.

OWEN: I told you, Mitchell caught me going out of the building. I was on the way.

BROOKE: Sure.

He sighs.

We had one chance to make a first impression. You left me hanging and I blew it. You know what? I don't think you even want a kid.

OWEN: That's not fair. I do so.

BROOKE: Doesn't seem like it.

OWEN: You sprang this plan—this whole other person—on me. We're still trying to have a child together.

BROOKE: We are trying to make my body do something that it can't and it's hurting me—

OWEN: Please, babe, don't. You don't know that—

BROOKE: I *do* know it! I *feel* it!

OWEN: *(Holds out his arms for her. She does not accept.)* You can feel something really strongly but that doesn't mean it's physically impossible—

With a certainty and a ferocity we have not seen from BROOKE thus far.

BROOKE: No, you stop that! Stop gaslighting me! What if feelings and data are NOT two separate things at all? And what if, Owen, the world is not just a big fancy switchboard with a series of levers and buttons and toggles that you can yank on until you get the outcome you want, huh? What if that?

Pause. This is new. He absorbs.

OWEN: *(Beat.)* You have your heart set on this?

BROOKE: *(Fierce.)* Yes.

OWEN: Okay, I hear you. I want to make you happy, Brooke. But no one makes good decisions under pressure.

BROOKE: That's the only way decisions get made. This was a real opportunity and, damn it, it was important to me.

After a moment.

OWEN: I told you, I was on the way.

Pause, she is not having it.

This young woman you met—tell me about her.

BROOKE: Well, she's freaked out—who wouldn't be? But she's really interesting, tough, smart, *funny*. A ton of character.

OWEN: You got all that in one sitting?

BROOKE: I am what, Owen, if not a good judge of character?

OWEN: Point taken. A worker, though. And what about the father? Is he in the picture?

BROOKE: I don't think so.

OWEN: It's just all so messy.

BROOKE: *(Beat, then suddenly.)* "To solve an intractable problem, you suspend two contradictory principles to an infinite point until they yield a solution."

OWEN: Who is that? Who are you quoting?

BROOKE: You.

She's kind of got him, but he does not want to admit it.

OWEN: Yes, but—

BROOKE: Like maybe A: you're going to blow us all to kingdom come on the one hand...Or B: You're going to invent a benign power source and save humanity on the other.

Holds out both hands.

OWEN: Now you're mocking me?

BROOKE: I'm not. I know you are *far* more likely to go for option B. And I am here for that party. Like every day with you, Owen, it's like: Wake up and believe six impossible things before breakfast. I do that for you. But you won't do it for me.

OWEN: I'd do anything for you. Everything I'm doing is for you. For us.

Pause; she does not answer immediately.

BROOKE: Except the only thing that matters.

OWEN: That's not true.

She shrugs, or is silent, whichever is worse.

It's not.

Again, as above.

Okay.

BROOKE: *(Carefully.)* Okay what?

OWEN: If it means that much to you, set it up again, we'll meet her.

Grabs her phone.

BROOKE: Really? Okay! *(Texting.)* "Hello Iona." What should I say?

OWEN: Just let her know I got held up and that we'd like to reschedule.

Bloop. She has sent a quick text, but there is no immediate response.

BROOKE: She got it, but she's not answering.

OWEN: She's behind the wheel. Do you want the maybe mama of our future child to be texting while driving a loader?

BROOKE: Right! I just hope I didn't blow it already. I got nervous, started blathering on. When I offered to reimburse her for lost wages, she got the weirdest look.

OWEN: *(Trying to be casual.)* You offered her money, you said. How much?

BROOKE: Like I was the wicked witch in a fairy tale coming to snatch away the child.

OWEN: How much did you offer her?

BROOKE: Oh, just housing, food and lost wages. She can't lose a year's pay for carrying our child, right?

OWEN: No, but Brooke, we have to be careful here.

BROOKE: I was trying, but how could I know that offering to cover someone's wages could be misconstrued?

OWEN: I mean careful with money. Until we're cleared for another round of research and development, things are…tight.

BROOKE: How tight?

OWEN: We'll be fine, I think. Just right now I am playing a little bit of the old shell game. Everyone is.

BROOKE: Actually, you know what? Don't tell me right now. Can we just go to sleep?

OWEN: All right.

She turns off the light, then after a moment in the darkness, changes her mind, turns it on.

BROOKE: Okay, how bad is it?

OWEN: We're not out on the street. Never mind, I'll handle it.

BROOKE: We'll handle it together.

Pause.

OWEN: "Two contradictory principles suspended to an infinite point..." Damn, woman, you are good.

BROOKE: Thank you.

OWEN: I love you. *(Beat.)* You love me back. You can't help it.

BROOKE: I do.

OWEN: Don't try.

BROOKE checks the phone again, nothing. She puts it beside her on the bedside table. A small pause.

BROOKE: Love you, too.

Scene 2 *(750 clicks)*

IONA storms over to the campfire. HORT is having a smash.

IONA: What the actual fuck, Hort?

HORT: Before we embark on any discussion, I have to warn you that I am about three sheets to the wind right now.

IONA: What are you doing? It's Tuesday.

HORT: *(Squints at the bottle.)* Make that three and a half.

IONA: You said you'd drive me!

HORT: Shit, right. I can snap around here. Let me get a sandwich.

He puts the drink down, rummages in cooler, slaps together a sandwich, eats it through the scene.

You drive for a couple hours then we'll switch.

IONA: For fuck sakes, did you have to spill your guts, Hort?

HORT: Justin put me in a submission hold.

IONA: Our Justin?

HORT: Yeah, I never seen him like that. Threatened to cut off my balls with a buck knife.

IONA: Like hell.

HORT: Okay, radical truth?

IONA: I got time for nothing else, son.

HORT: Well, I considered your request to keep this a secret. But I found it an infringement of his free will…

IONA: Aren't you the king shit, sitting there debating ideas? It's not his damn life on the line, nor yours.

HORT: Fair point. At first, I saw you upset, and agreed to keep it from him. But afterward I thought about what this might do to him, to our friendship. That seemed the greater evil.

IONA: I told you not to!

HORT: You did.

IONA: And you promised!

HORT: *(Nods.)* One of my character flaws. Very unreliable.

IONA: He won't stop hounding me. He's all messed up in his head, now. He'll screw up his own life, too.

HORT: He may. And you probably think I am an asshole.

IONA: Think it? Old son, I know it!

HORT: But I am a principled asshole.

IONA: *(Oddly calm.)* I'm going to kill you.

HORT: That's human existence. We have to stand in the full force of the blast to be fully alive, Iona.

IONA: *(Considering.)* I actually think I may kill you.

HORT: Wouldn't blame you.

IONA plops down in the camp chair.

Well, come on, aren't we going?

IONA: Yeah, in a minute…I don't know…No.

HORT: No? *(Eyes his drink.)* For sure, no?

IONA: No, for real.

He sits down, gets his drink, moves to offer her some, but if they aren't going she can't drink. He shakes his head.

HORT: I am so confused.

IONA: You and me both.

HORT: Look, you can't duck Justin forever. He's texting me every hour. You know he'll be back here right after rotation.

IONA: He's going to have to suck it up. He's not the one who'll lose his job.

HORT: No, but he *is* the one that could have a kid with a chip on their shoulder, a kid he never even knew existed, tapping him on his hairy neck in twenty years. You ever think about that?

IONA: Fuck.

HORT: If you are contemplating keeping it, you are going to need help. You got people?

IONA: I'm looking at him. A drunk in a camping chair grasping at straws.

HORT pulls himself to lucidity.

HORT: Hey, now. What about your family, wouldn't they—

IONA: My mother—

HORT: Go back home?

IONA: No, it would…she told me, not to end up like this. Barefoot and pregnant… *(Shudders.)* I'd rather die.

HORT: Have you tried talking to her?

IONA: It's just…not an option, Hort, okay? I have to help her, not the other way around.

HORT: Have the baby, then give it up for adoption.

IONA: *(Considering.)* I met this company woman, Brooke something from MARCOM. Did that *Blueprint for Tomorrow* thing. You know it? *(Beat.)* She and her husband can't have kids. They want to pay me.

HORT: Fuckin' A! How much?

IONA: A lot. About a hundred grand.

HORT: Holy shit! *(Whistles.)* If I had a babymaker, I know what I would do. There's actually a business model here. Pop out a few for them—you're set!

IONA: Hort, can we—

HORT: Think about it. That's life-changing money, Iona.

IONA: But what kind of a person does that make me?

HORT: A wealthier person.

IONA: My head is spinning, I can't think. What do you think I should do?

HORT: Buddy, I can cheer you on if you decide to raise the brat and live happily ever after. I'll applaud your smarts if you can sell it to some corporate shill...But the call? Well…you got to stare that one down alone.

IONA: *(Deep breath.)* Yeah. That's the problem.

Scene 3 *(man with a plan)*

JUSTIN and IONA are in The Rusty Bucket.

IONA: What do you want?

JUSTIN: Look, I shouldn'a gone off on you like that.

IONA: Like I'm not in enough shit? I need you piling on the guilt and shame?

JUSTIN: I know, I'm really sorry about that. It's not fair that this all falls on you. I been thinking and I have a plan.

IONA: Look out, here he comes, a man with a plan.

JUSTIN: Whatever brought us together that night... what I'm saying is that maybe everything happens for a reason.

IONA: Yes, there's a reason for everything, Justin, and the reason in this case is that we were both arseholed on cheap whisky and missing home.

JUSTIN: That's not what I mean.

IONA: What do you mean, then?

JUSTIN: Maybe we aren't perfect—and we don't know each other that well. But we have a chance to do the right thing for our baby.

He gets down on one knee. Oh no, he can't be doing this.

IONA: No, no way. And for fuck sakes get up off your knees.

JUSTIN: Will you marry me, Iona Macpherson?

IONA: Jesus wept.

He opens a box. There is a ring inside.

JUSTIN: I got this. I don't know if it's the right size.

He puts the ring box in her hand. She is dumbfounded and stares at the ring, in the fancy box.

IONA: This is like some kind of nightmare I had, but it's real. Are you really proposing to me in The Rusty Bucket? Get the fuck up, man.

JUSTIN: We can swap it in for something that suits you. The guy at the store said so.

She pulls him to his feet.

IONA: This must have cost you your whole paycheque.

JUSTIN: You only do this once; better get it right.

IONA: Stop it, you nut. We can't get married.

JUSTIN: We can too, we can do whatever we want! Come on, let's get out of here, you and me.

IONA: Justin…

JUSTIN: This place is evil. I say we go back home together. I'll get me a spot on the scallop line. It's up to sixteen bucks an hour now.

IONA: *(Shakes her head.)* That's it? That's the plan? After all this? It's back home to work the line at the fish plant?

JUSTIN: There's no shame in it. This place is the shits! Compared to this place, our little corner of the world is a piece of heaven.

IONA: You really do believe that, don't you?

JUSTIN: Yes. We can make a life together. A good life. Listen to me, now. I have been thinking about this a lot and, Iona, I never met a girl that I could just…hang out with. Say what I really think! Maybe that's what love is. Maybe love is just pillow fights and being able to speak your mind.

IONA: What about Caroline?

JUSTIN: Yeah. *(He looks down.)* Caroline. She's a really good person. She just…who's to know if she'd even want me now. I've changed since I've been here. I'm not the same man who left.

IONA: Yes, you are. To the guts of you, you are. You are so…decent.

Quietly, she considers what this life might look like.

You know, we might be happy for a while. Go home, get busy with a house and work and a baby and breakfast, lunch, dinner…And one day we finally get a moment's peace. You'll look out over the harbour and think, what in the hell have I done? *(Beat.)* Tell me I'm wrong.

JUSTIN: You don't know that.

IONA: I love you, you know, in a way—

JUSTIN: Goddamn it.

IONA: Just not the right kind of way.

JUSTIN: And what about the baby? I've lost so much, Iona. What if this baby is our chance to be a part of something—to do the right thing?

IONA: *(Gently holds out the ring to him.)* Go on and get your money back.

JUSTIN: Don't want the fuckin' money.

IONA: Take it, please.

He takes the ring back and throws it in his coat pocket.

JUSTIN: Fucking stupid thing.

IONA gets up to leave.

Please don't do this.

IONA: Goodbye, Justin.

She leaves. He wants to follow her but does not.

Scene 4 *(you don't get to cry)*

BROOKE and OWEN sit at a table in the pub waiting for IONA. BROOKE is fidgety, tapping her nails, checking her phone.

BROOKE: Ugh. It's ten past. She's probably not coming.

OWEN: Babe, take it easy.

BROOKE: Listen, when she gets here, can you...Be as critical as you want. Later. We'll get dinner, you can shred every nuance. But right here now, can you bring your A-game?

OWEN: By which you mean?

BROOKE: Uncomplicated. That dad that just wants to toss a ball around with his kid in the park.

OWEN: You want some generic jolly gent? *(Swings his elbows.)* Some cardboard cut-out man? I am just not that guy.

BROOKE: Can you *be* that guy? For an hour? For me?

OWEN: A half hour.

BROOKE: I'll take it. Anyway, I think you are that guy somewhere. Down deep.

OWEN: Very deep.

BROOKE is checking her phone, looking for IONA. She is not there yet.

BROOKE: Oh, I meant to tell you. Couldn't get to sleep so I read your proposal. The supporting docs, too.

OWEN: Did you? Bless your little pea-picking heart.

BROOKE: And...you're right about some things.

OWEN: Oooh, I like your opener. Say more.

She makes a face at him or sticks out her tongue, but it is done with warmth.

BROOKE: The reaction to the word is fear-driven. I mean, if you strip the word down to the root, it just means the centre of something.

OWEN: Yeah. We say nuclear family and no one freaks out. That's good, I'm making a note.

Takes out his phone, makes a voice memo.

Nuclear means the centre, the middle of things, the heart. Think nuclear family. Appeal to the future. Keep everyone warm.

He sees IONA enter, points with chin.

Ten o'clock, that your girl?

BROOKE: *(Turning.)* Yes. Now remember: uncomplicated. Baseball glove, on a Saturday. Affable! Put your phone away.

OWEN: Ready.

BROOKE: *(To IONA.)* Hi. Come and join us, please. Iona, I want you to meet my husband, Owen.

They shake hands. OWEN fakes a joke.

OWEN: Pleased to meet you, Iona. I'm Affable.

IONA: Hi. *(She gets that he's trying, but what?)* I thought you were Owen.

OWEN: Affable-Owen. One of those new-fangled double-barrel names.

BROOKE: *(Shoots him a look: zip it!)* An unavoidable work conflict delayed him last time and we are so happy you found time to meet with us again.

OWEN: *(A bit of joking gravitas.)* So happy. *(Looks around.)* Can we get you some lunch? Does this place serve food?

IONA: Nachos and hot dogs older than me. Nothing you'd eat.

OWEN: You're one of ours, I hear.

BROOKE: Iona is a Class 8 loader.

OWEN: Excellent. Really important work you are doing out there in the field.

IONA: Is it?

OWEN: Yes, the whole operation is nothing without the sum of its parts.

BROOKE: Truly, we value the contribution of every single employee.

IONA: I wish I was out there right now, truth be told.

OWEN: You like the work?

IONA: I like driving the rig. The sounds, the whistles, the size of the thing…It's a kick.

BROOKE: After the birth, you can be right back out there—

OWEN puts his hand gently on BROOKE's arm.

OWEN: Brooke, why don't we just see what she has to say.

Pause. IONA feels she should take the lead but is at a loss as to how.

IONA: You want *me* to talk? I don't know how this works.

OWEN: Iona, right? Beautiful name. You come from the East Coast, I hear?

IONA: Yeah.

OWEN: Beautiful part of the world. My great-grandfather came from there, on my dad's side. Went for vacation one time. Drove the Cabot Trail. Amazing seafood.

IONA: *(Nods, she's heard this one.)* Great fiddle music, too, I bet?

OWEN: We're here, *(Looks at BROOKE.)* as I understand it, to look for synergies.

IONA: What?

OWEN: To assess compatibility—

BROOKE: *(Jumping in.)* To see if we get along.

OWEN: Exactly. And if both parties agree we can put a contract in place.

He snaps open his case, pulls out a contract in triplicate.

This is an exemplar. I added in some riders about lifestyle choices, diet, exercise. We can amend as needed.

BROOKE grabs hers up, not pleased.

BROOKE: I didn't know you'd brought these along, Owen.

OWEN: I thought it would be helpful. If you surrender your child for adoption and if a couple were to adopt said child, this would be the type of document used.

IONA: If? *(To BROOKE.)* You two aren't sure?

BROOKE: No, we are sure.

IONA is looking at the contract. It is long and somewhat obtuse.

IONA: So this is, what? Like another job interview?

BROOKE: Not at all.

IONA: A test I have to pass? *(Reading.)* And you're going to tell me what to eat, and where I can go…You going to tell me what to think, as well?

BROOKE: Absolutely not.

IONA: Then I have to sign a contract—

BROOKE: You don't have to do anything you don't want to do.

OWEN: This protects you as well as us. So that in the event of a disagreement, a judge, say, could look at—

IONA: What judge?

BROOKE: He just means in the unlikely event—

OWEN: If either party were to change their minds once the baby is born—

IONA: So I would be stuck but you all could change your minds?

BROOKE: We won't do that.

IONA: Look, I can't be going to court. I can't afford lawyers. If I look you in the eye and say I'll do something, I'll do it! That's all I got.

OWEN: That's admirable. But the reality is that feelings can change once an infant arrives. What prevents you, theoretically, in the time leading up to the birth, from accepting help from a number of prospective parents?

BROOKE: Owen!

IONA: I hadn't even thought of that. *(To BROOKE.)* Is that what you would do?

BROOKE: Of course not. *(To OWEN.)* You're upsetting her—

IONA: I'm already in the shit. I cannot have people—*company people*—suing me!

BROOKE: We're not going to sue you! Frig, Owen. *(Beat.)* We want to lay out a plan to help you get your life back on track. You would be comfortable all during the pregnancy. The child would be loved, cared for—they would want for nothing.

IONA: I bet.

BROOKE: After the birth, we could help you move back home, perhaps.

IONA: Why would I do that? It's a shithole. There's nothing back there for me. For anyone.

OWEN: Harsh.

IONA: Highest cancer rate in the country, worse than here. How's that for harsh?

OWEN: Where is that?

IONA: Used to be The Tar Ponds, but now it's called "Open Hearth Park."

OWEN: Very poor stewardship decisions were made there—

IONA: A thousand public hearings. Four hundred million dollars later, so they can tell us we're croaking from cancer. Thanks, guys.

BROOKE: I thought the site had been remediated.

IONA: Plant some grass over it, build a boardwalk and call it "green space." I'd have to admire the genius of it if yellow ooze wasn't still coming through the walls of my mother's basement.

BROOKE: Is your mother—

IONA: Never mind my mother! She's none of your goddamn business.

OWEN: Look, we are working on green solutions.

IONA: Keep telling yourself that. You, me, all of us up here are raping the land.

OWEN: Is that right? Do you know that every single energy company in the oil sands is also already working on renewables?

BROOKE: Take your voice down a bit.

OWEN: Do you even know the environmental footprint of a wind turbine?

IONA: No, but I do know that we're already fucked beyond fucked. *(To BROOKE.)* Why do you want to bring any more tiny humans to this hot garbage?

OWEN: Can you tell me how much tech waste comes from one solar farm?

IONA: No.

BROOKE: Stop it, I said.

OWEN: Do either of you understand that there isn't a magic switch to flip? What do you think happens if we step away from the controls up here? You think it gets better?

BROOKE puts her hand up to her head. She wants to stop this train but can't.

IONA is thrown by his barrage of facts, but no one bullies her; she braces up.

IONA: I know one thing. You have us, stupid Bluenosers, dumbass Newfies, poor people from all over the world, sitting out there freezing our asses off while you sit in the office and stick pins in maps. As long as we're desperate enough to haul our asses up north for work, we're all the same to you.

BROOKE: That's just not true.

IONA: Yeah? Then how come you rake in the real money while we sit in fifty below and watch our lives tick by in twelve-hour chunks? Make all the nice stories you want. Stink doesn't lie. I smell it sitting right here.

OWEN: We are providing thousands of people not just with jobs, but with careers.

IONA: Rip that straight out of a manual?

OWEN: With secure, dignified employment to feed their families.

IONA: Oh, right. *(To BROOKE.)* You wrote the manual.

BROOKE: If we could just reset here, I think—

IONA: Which one of you is firing blanks, anyway?

OWEN: *(Raises his hands in a firm stop gesture.)* I am not going to let you—

BROOKE: No, it's all right, Owen. *(To IONA.)* It's me. I'm the one who's…*(How to put it.)* broken.

OWEN: Don't, Brooke—

IONA: This isn't going to work.

IONA jumps up, pacing as if caged.

BROOKE: What do you mean?

IONA: You're offering me…what? Some cheap payoff? I need…to change my life. My whole situation.

BROOKE: Please sit down. You shouldn't be stressed out.

IONA: How in the name of sweet baby Jesus am I supposed to avoid that?

BROOKE: Because stress must be avoided—it produces cortisol and it goes right through the placenta to the baby—

IONA: By all means, let's protect the precious baby. Never mind the empty husk it comes out of.

OWEN: *(Stands.)* Brooke, let's go.

BROOKE: No, no. *(To IONA.)* I care about you.

IONA turns on BROOKE with sudden venom.

IONA: You're worse than him.

BROOKE: What do you mean?

IONA: Because you pretend to care. Like you pretend to care about the environment. It's all a con!

BROOKE: That's…that's not true, Iona.

IONA: All you care about is this, right? *(Points to her belly.)* Fine then, you want to buy a baby?

BROOKE: Please sit down.

IONA: Stop telling me what to do!

Let's call it what it is. I want…a half a million dollars.

OWEN: *(To BROOKE.)* There you go. Exactly what I was afraid of. Iona, I don't want to be crass, here—

BROOKE: Owen…

OWEN: Well, that's a ridiculous demand! And she's not conducting herself in ways that—

IONA: Oh, fuck off!

OWEN: Yeah? Well, let me put it to you like this. If we're going to pay for a surrogate, you don't seem like a very good investment.

BROOKE: You promised me—

IONA: You people…

OWEN: *(To BROOKE.)* See that?

IONA: Took a while to peel back the onion, but there you are. I see you: you're monsters.

OWEN gets between the two women.

OWEN: *(To IONA.)* You stop that. *(To BROOKE.)* Come on, honey, we're leaving.

IONA: You're going to sell a baby to monsters, you better get top dollar. The price just went up; I want a million.

OWEN moves toward the door.

OWEN: Are you coming?

BROOKE: *(Holds up her hand to OWEN.)* Owen, wait. Iona, I know you don't mean that.

IONA: Yes, I do.

OWEN: Okay, I'm done. This is bullshit.

He leaves. BROOKE watches him for a minute.

BROOKE: Look, you're lashing out. You must be feeling so alone and so afraid—

IONA: I am not! If you knew what I already faced down in my life—Lady, you don't even know the half. I am not scared. I'm *pissed*.

BROOKE: Why?

IONA: That it's all on me. That I walked into this fucking trap.

BROOKE: You feel trapped?

IONA: Yes!

BROOKE: Maybe we can…think our way out of it…I do want to help you—not just the baby, but you, too.

IONA: Stop trying to play me.

BROOKE: I'm not! This baby, this child can be the greatest gift…to you, to us…

BROOKE has dropped her head into her hands sensing she is losing the battle, she begins to tear up.

IONA bangs on the table beside BROOKE.

IONA: No, you sit up! You stop that! You don't get to cry right now.

BROOKE: *(Wiping her eyes.)* I'm sorry.

IONA grabs her stuff.

IONA: This is no gift and I am not fucking Santa Claus!

IONA leaves. BROOKE is alone.

Scene 5 *(mr. lion rampant)*

JUSTIN has had the Nova Scotia flag tattooed on his back. HORT takes a quick look and makes a face.

HORT: Jesus Murphy, what did you get that stupid tattoo on your back for?

JUSTIN: I just wanted something…from back home. Something that I couldn't lose.

HORT: Looks infected. Guy change the needle?

JUSTIN: Of course he did. He's legit—he had a shop back home.

HORT: Oh, well then, a shop back home. That seals the deal for you? Did you *see* him change the needle? God knows what you caught, old son. I don't even want to think about it.

JUSTIN: I trust him.

HORT: And that will be your downfall.

He peeks again.

This is a mess. What is it even supposed to be?

JUSTIN: It's a lion rampant.

HORT: What's a lion rampant?

JUSTIN: The way he's standing. Upright, claws out, ready to strike. On a blue and white background? It's the goddamn Nova Scotia flag, you fool.

HORT: Okay…I see white, I see blue. But truth be told, I thought the middle part was pus. You best have it looked at.

JUSTIN: It's fine.

HORT: Come on, cheer up, Mr. Lion Rampant. Let's get shitfaced.

JUSTIN: How's that going to help?

HORT: Well, it never hurts.

JUSTIN: Nah.

HORT: *(Beat.)* I got to tell you something, man.

JUSTIN: What?

HORT: You're no fun anymore.

JUSTIN: Fun? With all that's going on, how can you be thinking about fun?

HORT: Because… *(He gestures to the camp, the world, everything.)* "all that's going on" ain't gonna stop. And fun…is all we got.

HORT passes the bottle. JUSTIN takes a swallow.

You know me, man. I might not be the richest asshole out here or the biggest or the strongest, but you know me.

JUSTIN: I know ya. *(Beat.)* Is there more? I was waiting for more.

HORT: We have been friends ever since we got off the tit and started tearing hell out of that little fog-soaked fish-guts town.

JUSTIN: Yeah.

HORT: In all that time, have I ever let you down?

JUSTIN: Yes. There was the time you left me in Digby.

HORT: I mean on something important.

JUSTIN: In a ditch.

HORT: Aside from that. I ever steer you wrong?

JUSTIN: That time we got the 4x4 stuck out on Maple Creek and I thought we should get a tow and you said just give 'er and we broke the crank shaft…

HORT: Okay, but—

JUSTIN: And I had to pay a thousand dollars I didn't have.

HORT: That was a fifty-fifty call. She could have just as easy come out.

JUSTIN: You told me to come up here.

HORT: You're missing the big picture—

JUSTIN: Now look at the state of my life.

HORT: Okay. What I am saying is that you can count on me to tell it to you straight. I am not going to sugarcoat it.

JUSTIN: No, that you don't do.

HORT: You have to let Iona do what she needs to, man.

JUSTIN: *(Shakes his head.)* What kind of man am I if I walk away from my child?

HORT: You won't win this one.

JUSTIN: It's not fair—

HORT: Who told you life was fair? Look, let Iona chart her own course. Whether she decides to get rid of it, or keep it, or sell it to that company woman, you don't—

JUSTIN: Sell it? What do you mean, sell it?

HORT: Shit. Man, let it go.

JUSTIN: To who?

HORT: She didn't say that's what she's gonna do. Look, Justin, Iona'll kill me—

JUSTIN jumps up, comes toward HORT.

JUSTIN: Not if I kill you first, Hort. What woman? What's her name?

HORT: I don't know. *(Beat.)* Blake, Brooke...or something. Married to one of the big shots at site. Look, she made me swear I wouldn't—

JUSTIN: Well, that's too bad. Are you my friend? Or not?

HORT: She made that training video. *Blueprint* something. That's all I know.

JUSTIN: *Blueprint for Tomorrow*. I remember. I'm gonna find her.

HORT: It's not your fight, Justin.

JUSTIN: Whose is it, then?

HORT: Maybe it's no one's.

JUSTIN: Like hell.

HORT: I'm telling you, man, no good will come of this. You got to let it go.

He tries to pass the bottle, JUSTIN bats it away and takes off. HORT shakes his head and takes another swig as the campfire flickers.

Scene 6 *(we're together or we're not)*

BROOKE is at the table, computer open, working. OWEN enters. They have not spoken since their meeting with Iona. She knows he is there but ignores him.

OWEN notices that she is not acknowledging him.

OWEN: Whew. That was a day.

Silence.

You eat yet? Getcha anything?

She shakes her head "no."

You're still pissed.

She pauses, considers. Says nothing.

Well?

BROOKE: Was that a question? I heard a statement.

He considers, then starts looking through work things on his phone. BROOKE snaps her computer shut.

It must be…so…comfortable to be you.

OWEN looks up. Oh shit.

(Thinks about it.) Forge ahead saying and doing exactly what you want. Smashing up people's lives, ripping up the earth. Who cares about the trail of chaos behind you.

OWEN: *(Warning tone.)* Brooke—

BROOKE: All under the banner of your almighty ideals. The bottom line, or jobs, or science. Or whatever fucking justification you give yourself to treat people like shit.

OWEN: Who's treating people like shit?

BROOKE: You are. Well, not all people.

OWEN: Oh, well then.

BROOKE: Just the ones who get in your way.

OWEN: All right. The fact is I have just as much of a right to be mad here. That girl insulted us—insulted you. You want me to stand by while a total stranger shits on you? Insults our relationship?

Full-on silent treatment.

I went to the meeting.

BROOKE: You came in with your nope face on.

OWEN: You want me to do backflips?

BROOKE: I wanted you to give it a chance.

OWEN: I asked a couple of simple questions.

BROOKE: A full-on inquisition! Contracts with riders in triplicate?

OWEN: Surrogacy is a complex agreement. If she can't handle a simple conversation—

BROOKE: You blew it up on purpose. And now we're never going to have our baby.

OWEN: Brooke! That's not— You have to stop this!

BROOKE: You get everything you want. It's not fair.

OWEN: You want to talk about fair? You of all people, Brooke—

BROOKE: Me?

OWEN: You've put me in an impossible position. Ask anyone about this plan of yours, they will tell you all the ways it will go south—

BROOKE: Yeah? How about you busting out the nukes?

OWEN: That is a completely, totally different—

BROOKE: Yeah, one is nurturing life and one is blowing it up.

OWEN: I'm not…Look, if we are going to raise a child together, we have to stick together. You didn't even leave with me.

BROOKE: You walked out. You didn't give her a chance.

He puts his hands up, like "Okay, let's find a compromise, here."

OWEN: Okay. Brooke. My beautiful wife, I get it. I am hearing you: this is a need, not a want. But this worker is not the right choice for us—

BROOKE: Her name is Iona.

OWEN: Okay, Iona might be—under different circumstances, maybe...But right now, she's...anyone becomes volatile if you twist their arm—

BROOKE: I am NOT twisting her arm! I'm helping! Owen, I am trying—

OWEN: *(Finishes her sentence.)* To get what you want.

BROOKE: No—

OWEN: Then what?

BROOKE: I was only...

She is so angry she can't finish the sentence, so he does.

OWEN: Playing to win. I'm sorry, Brookie. It's hard to hear—

BROOKE: I am the only one trying to salvage something in the middle of this fucking ruin.

OWEN: This *ruin*? Our life, you mean?

BROOKE: A couple years. I never agreed to sign my whole life away.

OWEN: You *wanted* to move here.

BROOKE: You know what they call this place? *(Nodding: they could be right.)* The asshole of the universe.

OWEN: We came here together. We've made every decision together—

BROOKE: Yet everything keeps coming out in your favour.

OWEN: That's not—

BROOKE: You get to go tinker! Problem-solve. Me? They call me when everyone gets upset, to patch things up.

OWEN: Your work is important, too, Brooke.

BROOKE: "Too." Do you even hear yourself? I have taken so much shit. Do you have any idea what it's like to be the one they call when everyone is screaming for blood? No. You're out in the field flying around in helicopters and collecting soil samples. Getting slapped on the back by your pals in the lab.

OWEN: Look, we can't adopt a baby from a worker. It's too messy.

BROOKE: Let's talk about messes. Not one of those tailing ponds...I mean, we have been dumping that shit for fifty years, and not *one* site has been remediated.

OWEN: You're getting me all wrong—

BROOKE: And if you get these state-of-the-art nuclear reactors that you've got such a hard-on for, who gets the radioactive waste? Maybe cleaning up the "messes" is exactly what we're put on earth to do.

OWEN: Be reasonable, Brooke.

BROOKE: No, you be fucking reasonable. There is no way that I am going to sit here and let you speak to me like this when I am the only one trying to save our baby.

OWEN: STOP SAYING "OUR BABY"! For the love of god.

BROOKE: Fine, *my* baby then.

OWEN: What…are you saying? You'd go ahead, and have a child without me?

BROOKE: I don't want to. I'm trying to explain…

OWEN: You would choose some gold-digging stranger—

BROOKE: She's not—

OWEN: Some low-skills opportunist? She called us *monsters*, by the way. She's just looking to make a buck—

BROOKE: FUCK YOU.

OWEN: Fuck me? Fuck you!

BROOKE: Don't say that about her! You don't even know her.

OWEN: NEITHER DO YOU. THAT'S MY POINT. You are not to give her anything out of our shared accounts.

BROOKE: You can't tell me what to do.

OWEN: I'm warning you, this is too much. I can't… You have to stop.

BROOKE: Why are you making this into an ultimatum?

OWEN: HOW IS IT NOT AN ULTIMATUM? Okay, then. You need to make me the bad guy?

BROOKE: You're doing a bang-up job of that all by yourself.

OWEN: Fine. Okay, then choose.

BROOKE: *(Clarity.)* I…am doing this, Owen.

OWEN: Really? *(He is in shock.)* Unbelievable. What we've been through…I don't want to lose you—

BROOKE: I want…I need to be a mother. Can't you understand?

OWEN: I can, but not like this.

He gets up, quietly gets his things, he is leaving.

BROOKE: *(Absorbs this.)* Oh. Owen, don't go.

OWEN: I…love you so much, Brookie. More than anything, but…

BROOKE: Please?

OWEN: This is over my line. I can't.

BROOKE: If you change your mind, Owen…If you do, I'm right here.

Scene 7 *(people like you)*

JUSTIN is waiting outside the offices with an unlit cigarette. BROOKE comes out of the building. JUSTIN calls out to see if he has the right person.

JUSTIN: Hey, *(Using it as a nickname.)* "Blueprint for Tomorrow," got a light?

BROOKE: *(Looking around.)* Excuse me?

JUSTIN: You're Brooke Adams. You made that video, right?

BROOKE: I worked on it, yes—

JUSTIN: Well, I'm here to tell you what a steaming crock of shit that was.

BROOKE: Noted. Thank you for your…feedback. Now, if you don't mind—

JUSTIN: Justin Covey, the father of the baby you're trying to buy.

BROOKE: Oh, for the love of— Listen to me, there has been a misunderstanding—

JUSTIN: Misunderstanding, my left nut! I thought I had seen some badness in my day, but this is the limit. It's filthy! It's wicked! You can't buy a baby.

BROOKE: We are not— Okay. So I take it you are Iona's partner?

JUSTIN: That's none of your goddamn business.

BROOKE: Trust me, I really don't want it to be, and yet here you are, insisting.

JUSTIN: We're not "partners." Iona didn't even have the decency to tell me! I had to hear it from Hort.

BROOKE: *(Tired, trying.)* Hort?

JUSTIN: My best friend. Or so I thought.

BROOKE: I'm just trying to understand what's going on here.

JUSTIN: You and me both!

BROOKE: Can I ask you to bring your voice down just a notch—

He braces himself up, he has never faced off with someone like this in his life.

JUSTIN: No, I will not. I'm the father and no matter if you're all trying to keep me in the dark, I have rights!

BROOKE: Unless a woman names you as a parent, you are not a father. In fact, she's not legally bound to make you aware of the pregnancy.

JUSTIN: Well, now that I have, as you so nicely put it, been made aware...What am I supposed to do?

BROOKE: I don't see that you need to do anything.

JUSTIN: What? Walk around the earth knowing I am a father but I'll never meet my child?

BROOKE: Being a father isn't just genetic material.

JUSTIN: I know that!

BROOKE: It's accepting full financial, physical and emotional responsibility for a child.

JUSTIN: I can do that.

BROOKE: Giving them a safe, stable home.

JUSTIN: And you assume because I'm under your boot that I can't give it?

BROOKE: If you're under someone's boot, it isn't mine.

JUSTIN: You think just because I'm twenty-five and you're some old scow you can lecture me on what it takes to be a father. I lost mine. He gave his life trying to scrape a living off the bare sea bottom after people like YOU sold him out.

BROOKE: People like me?

JUSTIN: Yes, people like you: Rich people.

BROOKE: That's not—I'm not a *rich person*.

JUSTIN: Well, I *been* poor and you sure as shit aren't that. You buy our backs, you buy our time, and now you think you can buy the next generation as well?!

BROOKE: This conversation is over, Mr. Covey.

She tries to step away, but he walks with her.

JUSTIN: What makes you think you are any more fit to raise a child than I am?

BROOKE: I never said that.

JUSTIN: Did you or did you not offer Iona money?

BROOKE: If a woman chooses to be a surrogate, she can be compensated—

JUSTIN: You think you can because you're management, and I'm a rig pig—

BROOKE: That has absolutely nothing to do with it.

JUSTIN: It has everything to do with everything! We're not done here.

He grabs her arm. She looks down at the arm, quietly.

BROOKE: You cannot just accost somebody in the street—

JUSTIN: I'm not accosting. I'm telling you to your face.

BROOKE: I heard you. Now take your hands off me.

She shakes off his grip, firmly.

Step back this minute and do not contact me again.

JUSTIN: Or what? You'll sue me?

BROOKE: I might. Try me!

He steps back but does not drop his point.

JUSTIN: Fine. But I'm telling you: Over my dead body will I let you or anyone else BUY MY BABY.

He leaves. She looks after him, suddenly very, very sad.

Scene 8 *(can you hear me now)*

IONA is on her phone with earphones in. We only hear her side of the conversation. She is walking around, trying to get better reception for the call.

IONA: Hey, Ma? Can you hear me? What about now? WiFi is the shits out here. There, you're back. What do you mean I never call you? I'm calling you now! Freezing my ass off to do it. Listen, I have something I need to ask you.

Clunk. Her mom has dropped the phone.

Oops, lost you. Were you sleeping? Ma, can I ask you a thing? Like, you are such a badass in all those old pictures. Oh, I know, you still are. But, like, what would you have done if you hadn't had me? *(Beat.)* No, just what if? Would you have travelled the world, or learned to build houses *(Beat, listens.)* Totally. Yeah.

Listens.

I know. But I just want to know…was it worth it? Ma? Can you hear me? Ma?

Her mom is medicated, drinking or both. Lots of words come from the phone, not good words. IONA reacts, pacing, moving her body, almost as if the words are jabbing her.

Mom, can you not please. ... Look, can you give a call over to Winnie's? I know you don't need help. I'm just saying—

Her mom cuts her off with something along the lines of "I don't know why I am alive, anyway."

Don't. Don't say stuff like that, okay, don't, please? Stop.

She rips the earbuds out of her ears, throws them.

FUCK!

Changes her mind, scrambles to find them and stuffs them back in her ears.

Ma? Ma, I'm sorry. *(Listens.)* Yeah. Okay... No, I know you are...What? Say again. *(Beat, listens.)* No, never mind. Get something to eat, okay? How's the leg? Get it looked at. I'm gonna send you another e-transfer. You have to take care of that. Promise me, okay?

Listens.

Me? Oh, I'm good. You know, hell froze over and I'm in it. What's the plumber's motto again? Shit flows downhill and payday is on Friday. Nah, Mom...Really, I'm good...Gotta go...Heading to work...Bye.

She sinks to the ground. Alone alone alone. As she looks out over the torn-up landscape, she hugs herself around the belly.

Scene 9 *(kind of fucking noble)*

HORT at the campfire. JUSTIN enters, upset.

HORT: Get over here and take a seat. Cool your jets, son.

JUSTIN: She wouldn't listen, so I just grabbed her arm—

HORT: You touched a company woman? Jesus, Justin, what are you thinking? If they come for us, it won't be Constable McDoohickey from down the cove. There'll be no, "sleep it off, son" and a slap on the wrist. You get in these people's way, they will fuck up your shit for life.

Pause, JUSTIN takes this in.

JUSTIN: I know it. I just...You seen Iona?

HORT: Not in the last twenty-four. Leaving her some space—and so should you.

JUSTIN: How can I?

HORT: You got no choice. Now pass the rum, Mr. Lion Rampant.

He points to the tattoo on JUSTIN's back.

That tattoo heal up yet?

JUSTIN: Leave it, Hort.

HORT: No, seriously. I was just getting at you. Let me get a look at it.

HORT leans over pretending to exam it, then slaps him, a little too hard.

JUSTIN: Ow! Fuck off.

HORT: Well, it's going to look some damn stupid when you get back. What's so great about back home anyway?

JUSTIN: Maybe it's not perfect—

HORT: You know what people are going to say before they open their mouths. Everything stays exactly the same.

JUSTIN: Maybe things stay the way they are because some of it—I'm not saying all of it—but some of it is good and kind of fucking noble or something.

HORT: Go on, tell me about how you should go back home and carry on the great tradition of our forebearers.

JUSTIN: Well, I might. I just might.

HORT: Been nice knowing you. If the bank don't get ya, that cold bitch the Atlantic will.

Pause. JUSTIN passes the bottle but does not take the bait.

Never be able to get your own licence. Be a deckhand your whole life. Till your back gives out or the captain cuts you loose for the cost of the gear. Another dumb boy gone under the waves.

JUSTIN: You're talking about my friends and family! You dumb fuck.

JUSTIN tackles HORT hard, knocks him off his chair. His drink goes flying.

HORT gets up and grabs Justin. They are fighting, not with cheap punches but in the way people do when they love each other.

HORT: *(As close to an apology as HORT gets.)* All right, you made your point. I was out of line.

JUSTIN: Asshole.

HORT: You done pounding on me yet?

JUSTIN: Nope.

JUSTIN is tired but gives him another couple of shots. They still have a hold of each other.

HORT: You done now?

JUSTIN: Guess so.

HORT: *(With tenderness.)* All right, old son, I got to tell you. You're just not cut out for it up here. You better go home. You have the whiff of a man who wants his slippers and his fireplace.

JUSTIN: It's all so fucked up.

HORT: Just go the fuck home, okay?

JUSTIN: Get off me.

HORT: You let go.

JUSTIN: You first.

They finally let one another go. In this letting go, JUSTIN accepts that this might be his best path. Pauses a moment.

How am I going to face Caroline? …

HORT: Don't bother her with any of this.

JUSTIN: How's that, now? Mr. Radical Truth?

HORT: Won't help her make a life with you.

JUSTIN: Nope. *(Beat.)* But what if Iona has the baby… and one day they're all grown up and they track me down.

HORT: Well, that could happen. You could have some kid come pull up in your yard for answers… Just try not to be an asshole if it happens.

JUSTIN: *(Absorbing.)* Jesus, Hort…

HORT: That's your cross to bear. Now listen, I'm locked down here for another ten weeks, but I'll be goddamned if I will spend Christmas at the North Pole, so when I get back home, I am gonna need a place to crash. Justin, you hear me? I'm gonna need to borrow your truck.

JUSTIN: *(Pulling himself together, what else can he do?)* Yeah, yeah. Okay.

They straighten up their hoodies and hats. HORT pounds JUSTIN on the back.

Scene 10 *(strong as a mother)*

IONA and BROOKE are back at the bar.

BROOKE: Thanks for coming, Iona.

IONA: You are apparently not one to take no for an answer, so…

BROOKE takes out an envelope.

No, keep it. The baby is not for sale.

BROOKE: This isn't…contingent on anything—you don't have to give me the baby. I just want to…help.

She pushes it over to her.

There's some info in there you might need. Company resources, provincial programs…

IONA looks inside.

IONA: And a cheque for ten grand?!

BROOKE: To buy you some breathing room. Just take it.

IONA: So I get up…walk out of here. And we never see each other again?

BROOKE: Yes.

IONA: I don't need your charity.

BROOKE: That's not what this is.

IONA: What is it then?

BROOKE: A gift? It doesn't matter.

IONA: A gift? So you're Santa Claus now.

BROOKE: *(Tired suddenly.)* Sure.

IONA: Well, I'd have to be a fool not to take it.

BROOKE: Just one thing.

IONA: Here we go.

BROOKE: No. *(Beat.)* Iona, will you accept my apology? You see, I wanted…I wanted so very much to have my own…

She can't finish; IONA finishes for her.

IONA: Baby. You can say the word. You wanted your own baby. People do. It's not a crime.

BROOKE: I told myself it was fate made our paths cross.

IONA: Fate. Otherwise known as Stephanie from HR.

BROOKE: *(Acknowledges.)* Yes. And I saw someone…I saw you, Iona, in a perilous situation. And I tried to play the advantage.

IONA: Everyone does that.

BROOKE: Well, they shouldn't. How do I know if you should carry a baby to term and give it up?

IONA: *(Quietly, finally someone gets it.)* And what if I give them up for adoption, and they never forgive me?

BROOKE: Or blame the ones who raise them. If you want an abortion, there's not a bit of shame in it.

IONA: *(Nods.)* But what if…this baby is the best thing that will ever happen to me, but I can't see it?

BROOKE: Could be.

IONA: But every waking moment goes to making enough money to survive. If I go back home, I'll disappear into a pile of dirty diapers and bitterness…The last anyone will ever see of me—the real me, anyway.

BROOKE: Is that what you think of the woman who raised you?

IONA: NO! She is strong…like iron, you know?

BROOKE: So are you. And I want to tell you one thing: You'll be strong, as a mother, if that's what you decide to do.

IONA: You don't know that.

BROOKE: I have very good instincts about people. My one superpower. *(BROOKE begins to gather her things to go.)* You're going to be okay, Iona. I am glad I met you, and please forgive me for whatever chaos I caused in your life.

IONA: Wait. Don't leave.

BROOKE: What is it?

IONA: I need…

BROOKE stops, listens.

To hit pause, or…I came out here because I wanted some control, you know? It sounds childish…

BROOKE: Go on.

IONA: It's so fucking hard. Everyone sees you as a piece of meat, or a set of hands. I finally make a friend, someone who really has my back. *(Beat.)* You know how when you are so super sad you just need to feel another body?

BROOKE: Yes.

IONA: We slept together, wrecked everything. *(Shakes her head.)* So stupid.

BROOKE: One Justin Covey?

IONA: Yeah…How—

BROOKE: He was waiting for me outside of work the other day with some pretty strong feelings.

IONA: Oh, god.

BROOKE: But you were super sad, you said. Why?

IONA: Back home your life is pre-mapped. You marry a fisherman, and if you're lucky he does not hit. Have a kid, work in the fish plant, stand all day on cold concrete just to pay the bills, and the cycle repeats. I wanted out.

BROOKE: You got out.

IONA: But I can't go to site with a belly out to here. I'm a joke. I'm screwed.

BROOKE: You're still the one in the driver's seat.

IONA: I'm fine in the truck, tunes blasting. But here in the real world, I'm the shits.

BROOKE: That's not true.

IONA: It is! All I do is hurt people.

There is a pause, both women consider.

BROOKE: You have the right to make yourself happy. Has no one ever told you that?

IONA: You'd…be the first.

BROOKE: You do.

IONA: I don't mind hard work, but I want it to mean something. We are making a huge mess. Who is going to clean that up?

BROOKE: There are steps being taken to remediate and reclaim—

IONA: *(Don't shit me.)* Come on.

BROOKE: You're right. It's not enough.

IONA: When we're done sucking everything dry, then what? We walk away and leave it?

BROOKE: We can't—

IONA: I am not someone who walks away. But you and your husband can give the baby opportunities that I can never—

BROOKE: My husband and I are not on the same page on this matter.

IONA: What does that mean?

BROOKE: He might not be involved.

IONA: You're splitting up? Because of me!

BROOKE: Splitting up, no. We have a strong bond. Strategies for managing differences.

IONA: As big as this?

Pause. Big breath from BROOKE, she hadn't fully considered this loss yet, but does now.

BROOKE: I'm not sure.

Pause.

IONA: Have you ever even looked after a kid?

BROOKE: A few times. Not for long.

IONA: I have, and they take *everything* you've got. Your life will be unrecognizable.

BROOKE: I think that's…a good thing.

IONA: You say that, but you have no idea. *(Beat.)* See? I told you. Everything I touch turns to shit.

BROOKE: Don't say that.

IONA: It does. What am I going to do?

BROOKE: I don't know, Iona. What do you want to do?

They sit in silence.

IONA: What if...I don't disappear? What...if I help?

BROOKE: Help whom?

IONA: You.

BROOKE: What does that mean?

IONA: What if you could be the one who gives her a home and I could still...What if I—

BROOKE: The baby...is a girl?

IONA: I don't know, I haven't had an ultrasound. It's just a strong feeling. Anyway, the important thing is she'd have a roof over her head and food on the table and she'd be safe. You can do that, right?

BROOKE: I can if...you are sure that's what you want.

IONA: I don't know. Maybe I could go to school or maybe I could travel. I can't marry some guy for a paycheque. I *don't* want to abandon this baby, but I do want to be the mom, I think. One thing I do know is I don't want to be stuck. I can't —I'll lose it.

BROOKE contemplates this.

BROOKE: So...if I hear you correctly, I commit to parenting, providing for the baby, but you would want to be "Mom"...like an open adoption situation.

IONA: Ah...that's not fair, is it?

BROOKE: Fair to whom?

IONA: You.

BROOKE: Maybe so, maybe not. But I know what I'm getting into. And what if I'm not…the most important person here? She is and you are, too. *(Coming to a decision.)* I want to do this.

IONA: Holy shit, really?

BROOKE: Yes.

IONA: If we do, we'll be linked…forever. A kid is for keeps.

BROOKE: That's right, for keeps.

IONA: People…won't understand, they won't get it at all—

BROOKE: *Fuck* those people.

IONA: It goes against the way things work.

BROOKE: The way things work is broken. Especially here.

IONA: What about the last name? What do we write on the forms?

BROOKE: What do you want to write?

IONA: What if I want to get out of here?

BROOKE: Like, for a while?

IONA: Or for good?

BROOKE: I'll have to find another job. Another place to live. I guess we'll have to…figure it out.

IONA: Holy shit. But what about when it gets hard? What if we don't agree on things?

BROOKE: Isn't that what happens to everyone raising kids?

IONA: What if you change your mind?

BROOKE: I'm not going to change my mind. Like you said on the day we met: "If I look you in the eye and say I'll do something, I'll do it."

IONA: Okay.

BROOKE: We can make up some agreements and things if you want them, but I give you my word.

IONA: You won't abandon her?

BROOKE: Never. Nor you.

IONA: What about your husband?

BROOKE: *(Considers this.)* When he cools off, he'll get some clarity. He'll see this baby and you are the best things that could happen to us. And he'll come back.

IONA: Are you sure about that?

BROOKE: *(Admits.)* I am not sure, but I…have hope.

IONA: This so messy…so wild…

BROOKE: Maybe beautiful, too?

IONA: Messy, wild, and maybe beautiful.

BROOKE: Like family.

IONA: That sounds about right.

BROOKE reaches for IONA tentatively. IONA hurls herself at BROOKE, clenching her in a rough hug that says "Yes."

End of play.